From Frankie Solarik—the visionary behind Toronto's critically acclaimed BarChef bar, and judge on Netflix's international hit competition show *Drink Masters*—comes a book to challenge any preconceived notions of what a cocktail can be.

Dubbed a "legendary Toronto experimentalist" by *The New York Times*, Frankie is revered around the world for his modernist cocktails. His famed cocktails are all-encompassing culinary experiences that combine top-of-the-line spirits, molecular gastronomy, and edible components. With *Modernist Cocktails*, professional and home mixologists alike can try their hand at his multisensory creations. Inside these pages you'll find:

Masterpiece cocktails: Assembled by season, Frankie's landmark recipes translate nature's narratives into spectacular drinks served within evocative set pieces—taking inspiration from winter's thaw into spring, a summer sunset's glow, or the colorful turning of autumn's leaves.

Inspired sips: For every modernist cocktail recipe, there are three additional simple sip recipes drawing inspiration from similar ingredients within a much simpler presentation—these are quick-assembly drinks to return to night after night.

Leading-edge techniques: Learn molecular methods like spherification, cryogenics, how to craft flavored airs and foams, and more.

Home-crafted essentials: Elevate your bar with homemade bitters, infusions, and syrups—must-haves when building cocktails of all levels.

This design-forward book with atmospheric photography situates you right at Frankie's bar, both serving and savoring these stunning drinks. Whether you shake and stir or sit back and sip, *Modernist Cocktails* is an enchanting welcome to a cocktail enthusiast's wonderland.

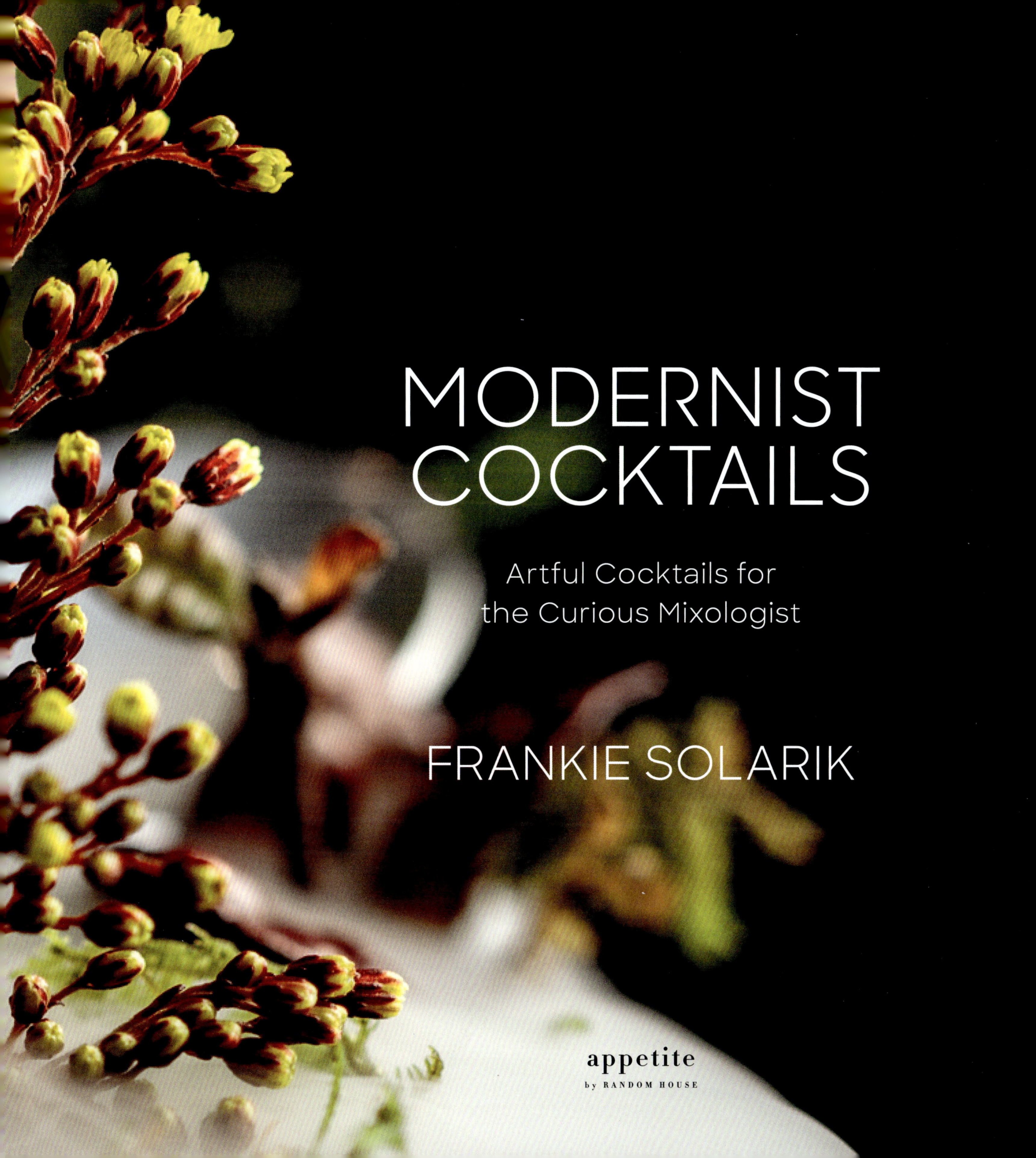

MODERNIST COCKTAILS

Artful Cocktails for the Curious Mixologist

FRANKIE SOLARIK

appetite
by RANDOM HOUSE

Library and Archives Canada Cataloguing in Publication is available upon request.
ISBN: 978-0-525-61308-4
eBook ISBN: 978-0-525-61309-1

Photography by Leanne Solarik
Image on vi (smoke): siaminka / Adobe Stock
Book and cover design by Terri Nimmo
Typeset by Daniella Zanchetta

Printed in China

The authorized representative in the EU for product safety and compliance is Penguin Random House Ireland, Morrison Chambers, 32 Nassau Street, Dublin D02 YH68, Ireland, https://eu-contact.penguin.ie

Published in Canada by Appetite by Random House®,
a division of Penguin Random House Canada Limited.
320 Front Street West, Suite 1400
Toronto, Ontario, M5V 3B6, Canada
penguinrandomhouse.ca

10 9 8 7 6 5 4 3 2 1

appetite by RANDOM HOUSE | Penguin Random House Canada

This book is dedicated to my family, to whom I'm forever grateful for being there for me throughout this journey: my dear wife, Leanne, who has supported me throughout my career; and my amazing sons, Kai and Lennox, who have taught me more than I would ever be able to teach them.

Contents

3.
SUMMER

4.
AUTUMN

5.
WINTER

barchef
Frankie Solarik

INTRODUCTION

Since the opening of the first BarChef location in 2008, my ambition has been to serve compositions that create what I call "the auditorium of perspective" for our guests. These cocktails, which emphasize a multi-sensory approach, have become our signature style. The idea is to create a micro-environment for guests, as if they are immersed in an IMAX theater experience through the cocktails' visuals, aromatics, textures, and fresh, unexpected ingredients that have been chosen with the utmost intent. After over 15 years, our goal at BarChef remains the same: to challenge the preconceived notions in the genre of mixology with our modernist cocktails.

The definition of modernist mixology has evolved drastically since its origins—it's even evolved since my first cocktail recipe book (*The Bar Chef: A Modern Approach to Cocktails*) was released just over a decade ago. In that book, I share only a handful of these modernist cocktail recipes, focusing instead on cocktails that are more minimalistic while still achieving distinct complexity. But, as mixology has developed, now feels like the right time to delve further into the world of modernist cocktails.

Even if you're well versed in the world of mixology—maybe you've sat at our counter at BarChef, or you're a home mixologist looking to elevate your repertoire, or you're developing your own professional bar program—it might be helpful to examine what I mean by a modernist cocktail.

First, I think back to the mixology space of the 1990s, when mixologists innovated classic cocktails like never before by using citrus juices and peels, herbs, and other fresh ingredients—instead of artificial juices dispensed from soda guns—and of carbonation techniques and foams. This was followed by the candied martini craze of the 2000s. Then with the 2010 era came the introduction of simpler culinary techniques—think in-house flavored syrups and craft ice. All this led to our present generation of mixologists: not only do we utilize culinary techniques of the past, we also incorporate progressive Michelin-starred-restaurant–quality techniques and ingredients (such as cryogenics, clarification, fat washing, and distillation, gelification, and aeration) in order to achieve amazing textures, flavors, and presentations.

And so: modernist cocktails follow this same ethos of progressive thought, advanced techniques, and attention to detail with garnishing techniques and various preparation methods. As in molecular gastronomy, modernist mixology uses innovative tools like refractometers and rotary evaporators, compressed carbon dioxide and liquid nitrogen—but rather than getting bogged down in the clinical nature of chemical reactions, modernist mixology finds inspiration in emotion. After all, while mixology following strict guidelines of proportions and exact ratios is certainly a science, it is important to remember that it is also an art.

I first began to view mixology from a different perspective while developing BarChef's inaugural cocktail program back in 2008. I was watching the documentary *Decoding Ferran Adrià*, hosted by none other than Anthony Bourdain. Chef Adrià is renowned for his work in molecular gastronomy, achieving international acclaim with his restaurant (run in collaboration with his brother Albert) and even garnering first place in the World's 50 Best Restaurants list for a record five times (to say nothing of placing second and third in other years). When Mr. Bourdain joins Chef Adrià for a tasting menu at El Bulli, I was enthralled by his reactions to the spherified green pea course: intrigue, delight, even a loss for words.

This was exactly the transformative experience I wanted to provide for my guests. Seeing the texture of liquid seemingly suspended without any casing in sphere form completely inspired me to approach this philosophy and see how these techniques could define my personal expression within mixology. It would involve manipulating commonly used ingredients to set their recognizable flavors in a contrastingly unrecognizable presentation, in pursuit of creativity, curiosity, and the chance to create an immersive scene for the guest. Right away, I ordered the ingredients and tools used in the video and soon found myself in my home kitchen at all hours of the day and night practicing and perfecting some of the techniques I had seen Chef Adrià employ, like spherification and creating light "air" textures using soy lecithin.

My approach has always been to incorporate emotion; through cocktails, I'm inspired to create art that is truly special, truly evocative.

Years later, I am thrilled to be considered the international reference of this modernist style of cocktails, and have been honored to share my passion both at BarChef and as a judge on *Drink Masters*. My approach has always been to incorporate emotion; through cocktails, I'm inspired to create art that is truly special, truly evocative. As well as through top-of-the-line tools and ingredients, the visceral experience comes together through visuals that accentuate a cocktail's flavors and aromas: textures, depth, gradient color, even techniques like illuminating the service piece from below can have an immense effect.

So, for my second book, I wanted to shine the spotlight on my modernist compositions and create a book meant to inspire thought, ideas, and a new sense of perspective. As professional mixologists and ambitious home mixologists, we must challenge the creative expressions of the past and create experiences for guests—whether at our place of work or home. These experiences tap into nostalgia and leave these people we care about with a new and lasting memory. And how better to do that than through complexly beautiful modernist cocktails?

The recipes in this book are divided into chapters that follow the seasons, emphasizing the beauty of nature, colors, inspiration, and emotion. Crafting these compositions will send you on a fascinating journey of modern mixology: you'll learn the ingredients, tools, and glassware with which to stock your bar (see pages 6 to 11), then, in addition to using multiple modern culinary applications (such as stabilization techniques that use cryo components like liquid nitrogen and dry ice, and gelification that uses agar and gellan gum), you will be guided through plating the service pieces for every cocktail, defining your own creative process all the way through execution. When I first created these recipes, I was often inspired by the unique plateware I was able to find; if you can't source the same piece, I encourage you to use dishes that inspire you!

Each modernist cocktail includes sub-recipes for its components—set yourself some time ahead of serving to prepare these. (The modernist cocktail's ingredients list is given in the order that each component is called for when plating, but be sure to read each component's own recipe to see whether it can be prepared ahead of time or whether it must be used immediately after making it.) These are then followed by "Inspired Sips": three simpler recipes that are a perfect way to enjoy these components and the syrups, bitters, and infusions you'll have stocked up on (see pages 15 to 21) while unwinding for the night. If you're new to creating modernist cocktails, Pastels of Violet (page 143) is a nice one to start with.

It's an amazing time to be a mixologist. With multiple means of access to information and references (like online tutorials and blogs, a variety of cocktail books, shows like *Drink Masters*, worldwide competitions, and mixologist takeovers at bars across the world so that guests can try different styles without needing to travel), the community and creativity in our industry have never been stronger. We have mixologists collaborating on ideas, and with the sum much greater than the value of its individual parts, we now see the fruits from years of this approach.

I write this book as my contribution to the community, with the intention of sharing my years and years of obsession with creating the ultimate transportive experiences for my guests, and inspiring the next generation of mixologists and chefs to carry on and challenge convention. After all, although this medium is about self-expression, in the end we must do what we do for others. So, I say to you what famous Argentine celebrity chef Francis Mallmann would say in these times of inspiration: "Keep the light lit!"

Frankie Solarik

THE EVOLUTION OF AN IDEA

Challenging convention—this is the key to creativity. To do anything truly groundbreaking, one must push creatively beyond the preconceived notions of the implied boundaries of your particular medium. Consider other disruptors in their field: Airbnb with the hotel industry, Uber with the taxi industry, Amazon with the retail industry.

In my case, this was the concept of the cocktail experience: I refused to be limited to the confines of the glass. Why not elaborate on this perspective, incorporating elements beyond the glass in ways that expand on each individual composition? This could mean anything from using a vessel that allows for edible components to accentuate the cocktail's flavors, all the way to designing your environment in a particular color or theme to create visual references that transport your guests while they enjoy your creations. Think sipping on a Negroni in a café designed to resemble the Galleria in Milan: Italian music in the background, furniture and design elements throughout the space all contributing to that transportive experience, thus emphasizing the visceral emotions that come along with the cocktail. Or how about a Hawaiian-themed bar with music of the region or the sound of the sea; tropical plants; aromatics of grilled pineapple, coconut, mint, and sunscreen; and lawn chairs on sand, the guests requested to remove their shoes upon entry and walk in the sand to feel its texture on their feet, the temperature in the room slightly warmer than expected. All this, of course, contributing to that transportive element and thus emotional connection to the cocktail experience. The possibilities truly are endless.

I sincerely believe that to be creative, one must allow themself to open up and be available to inspiration. It can arrive at the most unexpected times, and it usually leads to the best ideas.

Take, for example, the moment of creativity that sparked my modernist mixology journey and what would eventually become my signature cocktail for BarChef—the world's first smoked cocktail, the Vanilla and Hickory-Smoked Manhattan. I was watching an episode of *Iron Chef America* in which one of the chefs presented their dish to the judges using an upside-down ceramic bowl to conceal the food and maintain its temperature. To reveal the dish, the chef lifted the bowl and steam was released, cascading to the ground.

The spectacle of it all instantly inspired me to translate this technique to mixology. I wanted to create a smoked cocktail, but first, what to use to enhance flavors and create additional complexity in a non-astringent way (as smoke tends to add a level of dryness)? I began with a vanilla bean for its amazing aroma; however, it wasn't producing enough smoke on its own, and so hickory wood was needed to add more volume and structure to the aroma by contributing a large amount of smoke. The cocktail also needed additional levels of sweetness through accents of vanilla-infused cognac to balance the smoke. Even the vessel that would encapsulate all the smoke and the cocktail would be key to the experience. I decided on a glass vase, as I wanted my guests to be able to watch the smoke interact with the cocktail even before they drank it. Little did I know that this moment of innovative composition would allow me to place my individual stamp on the industry with the world's first smoked cocktail. The technique is now being used across the world. (You can learn how to do it yourself with the recipe in my first book, *The Bar Chef: A Modern Approach to Cocktails!*)

And so, how do you begin your journey with creativity and the joy of self-expression? The first rule of creativity: Don't look for it. You must trust and enjoy the process and allow yourself to be open to inspiration at all times. Be present. Stand in the middle of a forest, a city, a historic place, a museum. Observe the sights, sounds, textures, and aromas surrounding you. Take in Earth's seemingly effortless ability to create beautiful things: the visual complexities that we tend to overlook (such as the magnificent complex iridescent colors found in florals) are often the most impactful qualities. Music can also contribute to the sense of awareness and, of course, you can use it to create your own inspiration-enhancing environment. Choose music that relaxes you, motivating you in a calming way: classical, jazz, ambient house, it's your choice. Along with lighting (perhaps candles for a soft light) and aromatics (a lit piece of palo santo), I find this approach allows me to fixate on the tasks at hand and concentrate fully on the creative process.

Now your journey with creativity and your personal expression begins. Enjoy the process and leave your mark on this amazing industry!

STOCKING THE HOME BAR

Along with a progressive and contemporary approach to cocktails comes the need for a variety of kitchen and bar tools, equipment, and ingredients to push the possibilities of ingredient manipulation. The lists below cover all the essentials for making the recipes in this book. Specialty items can be found in kitchen supply stores or on specialty websites.

BAR TOOLS

ATOMIZER

A glass spray bottle used to provide a fine mist of liquids.

BAR SPOON

A spoon with a long stem, used for stirring cocktails.

BLOWTORCH

A small, portable device used to concentrate combustible heat, such as flames, to a specific area. Typically propane-based, these tools can generally be purchased at kitchen supply stores or hardware stores. Brûlée torches can also be used for smaller kitchen or cooking applications.

CANDY THERMOMETER

Also known as a sugar thermometer or pastry thermometer, this digital thermometer can read temperatures ranging from 150°F to 400°F (65°C to 200°C) or even higher. For the recipes in this book, it's the temperature of agar-based gels that you'll be taking.

CRYOGENICS

Below are the components necessary to safely use your cryo elements, like dry ice and liquid nitrogen.

Dewar flask: A specialized type of vacuum-insulated flask used to store material that must be kept below room temperature due to low atmospheric boiling points. You will use it for liquid nitrogen, which sublimates at any temperature above -321°F (-196°C), turning directly from a liquid to a gas.

Dry ice: Dry ice pellets are formed by carbon dioxide first being pressurized and then cooled into a liquid at a temperature of -109°F (-79°C) or colder. Dry ice must always be handled with the utmost care and while wearing protective gear (suitable gloves and protective eyewear), as it can be extremely dangerous. Never handle it with your bare hands or store in an airtight container.

When used properly, dry ice can produce amazing results in culinary applications, including snow-like textures. It is also useful for storing ingredients with high sugar or alcohol amounts. Dry ice can be sourced from licensed industrial gas suppliers.

Liquid nitrogen: Liquid nitrogen stores in its liquid state at -321°F (-196°C) in commercial-grade industrial insulated dewars. This ingredient must always be handled with extreme caution: always wear protective gear such as gloves and protective eyewear, as liquid nitrogen can burn you if not handled properly. Culinary applications for this remarkable ingredient include rapidly freezing ingredients with high fat, sugar, and/or alcohol levels—such as the branch component in Night Blossom (page 55)—or for interesting ice presentations like the rosemary ice found in Winter Storm (page 189). The reduced freezing time means smaller ice crystals are formed, which produce very smooth textures on the palate in the finished product. As with dry ice, liquid nitrogen can generally be sourced from licensed industrial gas suppliers.

Styrofoam container: An insulated Styrofoam container can be used to transport temperature-sensitive materials. In our case, it's excellent for holding dry ice or liquid nitrogen during preparation for any extended time, as it allows for ventilation and for built-up sublimated gases to escape.

DEHYDRATOR
A culinary device that removes moisture from food for preservation or, as with these recipes, manipulates its texture to that of paper, dust, or powder.

DEMISPHERE MOLD
A nonstick pastry mold with twenty-four 1-inch (2.5 cm) demispheres; in our case, used to prepare various pastry applications.

DIGITAL SCALE
A device used to achieve precise weights of small items or ingredients. In this book, some ingredients are measured to a fraction of a gram. Generally battery operated, these devices are extremely fragile and must be handled with care for the most accurate reading.

FOOD PROCESSOR
An electric culinary tool used to blend, puree, or chop solid ingredients into smaller-format applications. I recommend the Robot-Coupe, KitchenAid, and Breville brands.

HAND MIXER
A convenient portable electric mixing device with beaters to whip or mix a small amount of liquids. It's also excellent for aerating meringue.

HEXAGON MOLDS
Hexagon-shaped silicone molds, used to make the geometric cream gels. These can be found online by searching for puzzle molds, with each hexagon measuring about ½ inch (1 cm) in diameter.

IMMERSION BLENDER
Also known as a stick blender, this kitchen tool is used to blend ingredients, such as pureed food or juices. Its long shaft allows it to be submerged in liquids when preparing air components found in this book.

INSERT PANS (HALF, THIRD, AND QUARTER PANS)
These rectangular stainless-steel containers come in various dimensions and are used in the restaurant industry for storing ingredients and letting them set in configurations (like brunoise or bâtonnet). Generally 4 inches (10 cm) deep, the largest size is a whole pan, decreasing all the way down to a sixteenth. For the recipes in the book, I suggest getting half, third, and quarter pans. If you're having trouble sourcing them, you could substitute any equal-sized plastic or stainless-steel rectangular containers—look for them in kitchen supply stores.

ISI SIPHON AND NITROUS OXIDE CHARGER
Also known as a cream whipper, an iSi siphon is a canister that aerates cream-based liquids quickly into foams when used with pressurized nitrous oxide. To charge the iSi siphon with nitrous oxide, follow the manufacturer's instructions.

JIGGER
A device used by bartenders and mixologists to accurately measure small volumes of liquid when preparing cocktails. Jiggers can range from increments of ¼ oz (8 ml) to 4 oz (120 ml).

KING CUBE TRAY
Silicone, large-format ice cube molds that are generally 2 inches (5 cm) square or larger. Large-format ice cubes are excellent to reduce the rate of dilution in spirit-forward cocktails, so that the composition isn't overdiluted.

MASON JAR
A sealable glass jar used for airtight sealing and preserving of liquid-based ingredients. In this book, 34 oz (1 L) and 68 oz (2 L) jars are perfect for infusing accent liqueurs, bitters, and spirits.

MICROPLANE GRATER
A Microplane grater has small, sharp notches that yield especially finely grated results when used for grating citrus or spices.

MIXING GLASS
A 34 oz (1 L) glass or steel vessel will work well for these recipes, preferably with a spout for easy, no-spill pouring. Use this when stirring spirit-forward cocktails, to allow for appropriate dilution.

MORTAR AND PESTLE
Use this stone or ceramic tool to grind ingredients into a paste or dust.

MUDDLER

A wood, silicone, or stone pestle-type device for muddling ingredients, such as mint for a mojito, to incorporate their flavors when preparing cocktails.

OFFSET SPATULA

A palette knife–like tool often used in pastry applications. One with a 6-inch (15 cm) blade is perfect for handling the delicate gels or ice for the recipes in this book.

SPHERICAL ICE MOLD

A silicone spherical mold used to prepare ice components, generally 2½ inches (6 cm) in diameter.

SQUEEZE BOTTLE

A pliable plastic bottle with a small spout, which allows for precise application of ingredients. Look for bottles with a volume between 1½ and 5 oz (45 and 150 ml). The gels you make in this book are all stored in squeeze bottles, so keep a few on hand, as you might require multiple gels for one cocktail. The ingredients list of each cocktail will give you an approximate idea of how much you'll need for each; the method will then instruct exactly how many dots to squeeze.

STRAINERS

Chinois: A fine-straining device with a steel mesh fabric used primarily when extremely small pieces of an ingredient need to be removed from a large volume of liquid being poured into a cocktail glass.

Fine cocktail strainer: A small conical mesh strainer used for fine-straining and removing sediment from cocktails by setting it over the cocktail glass. It's often used in conjunction with a Hawthorne strainer, double straining to catch any bits that the Hawthorne doesn't. While it's similar in shape to a chinois strainer, a fine cocktail strainer is smaller, closer in size to a tea strainer.

Hawthorne strainer: A steel tool used to strain both shaken and stirred cocktails from their tin, keeping unwanted materials from entering the finished drink.

SYRINGE

A plastic device used to extract liquids with suction.

KEY INGREDIENTS

AGAR

Agar powder, or agar, is a gelification agent used in cocktails to achieve what's known as a "brittle gel," which, once set, can be blitzed to achieve various gel textures. It can also be used in very small proportions to clarify cocktails. Agar is generally activated around 203°F (95°C), depending on a liquid's boiling point or the sugar or alcohol ratios. Be sure to use a thermometer to achieve the temperature specified in the recipe.

ESSENTIAL OIL (ORGANIC FOOD-GRADE)

The recipes use essential oils to achieve defined and distinct flavors or aromas. In some cases, use these oils in extremely diluted amounts, and be sure to source oils that are organic and food-grade, so that they're safe to consume. These oils can generally be found online from essential oil suppliers.

GELATIN SHEET

Gelatin is by far a superior flavor-release gelling agent, readily available and easy to work with to create flexible gels. Gelatin thrives in applications where soft, chewy textures are desired, as opposed to the firm stiff gels made with agar.

GELLAN GUM

Gellan gum is used to create firm-textured gels. It also can be used to make instant fluid gels by blending it directly in liquids. A little bit goes a long way, so use sparingly.

Off
Low
High
Pulse

Xantana
Agar

SOY LECITHIN

Derived from soy bean oil during processing, soy lecithin is an excellent emulsification agent, binding flavors and ingredients. In our applications, soy lecithin is used to create air textures.

XANTHAN GUM

Xanthan gum is a powerful thickening agent, and very small amounts can instantly increase the texture of your chosen liquid. It is used in this book to increase viscosity.

GLASSWARE AND SERVING PIECES

AMBER STEMLESS COUPE

A glass bowl approximately 3 inches (8 cm) in diameter, generally between 6 and 8 oz (180 and 235 ml) in volume.

BENTO BOX

A ceramic, bamboo, or porcelain box, approximately 8 inches (20 cm) square and 3 inches (8 cm) deep, or 9 × 4 × 2 inches (23 × 10 × 5 cm). It is used in the recipes as a service piece and for presentation. You can find them in kitchen supply stores or homeware supply stores.

CHICKEN WIRE

Made with stainless-steel wire, which holds its shape when formed, chicken wire is used to create a stable base for certain cocktails in this book.

COLLINS GLASS

A tall cylinder-shaped vessel used to serve long-style cocktails that incorporate juices, sodas, or sparkling wines.

CRYSTAL COGNAC GLASS

A stemmed large-bowl glass used to accentuate the aeration of liquids with its large surface area.

DOUBLE OLD-FASHIONED GLASS

This is a large-format glass, generally built to hold between 14 and 18 oz (415 and 530 ml).

FLORAL FOAM

As in a professional plant arrangement, you will use this to fill space and provide support to various design materials in these modernist cocktails.

FOOTED CERAMIC BOWL

A ceramic bowl atop platformed feet, most often used for ornate displays or art pieces.

GLASS BOWLS

The recipes call for various styles of glass bowls: terrarium-style, abstractly shaped blown glass, tall cylindrical bowls. I encourage you to be inspired by this book's photography and find the vessel that works for each cocktail's needs.

LIVE SHEET MOSS

Foraged fresh sheet moss that can be purchased from wholesale florists. Spray with cold water and store in the fridge for up to 2 weeks.

RAMEN BOWL

A deep bowl generally used to serve large-volume soup.

STEMLESS GOBLET

A large round bowl glass that is used in this book to accentuate various ice components.

TULIP BURGUNDY GLASS

This stemmed wine glass has a large bowl with a fluted shape at the lip to accentuate and capture aromatics.

BITTERS, INFUSIONS, AND SYRUPS

Bitters, infusions, and syrups are all elements integral to achieving the flavor profile, complexity, and texture you're envisioning in a cocktail.

Bitters are traditionally used by mixologists in the same way a chef would use salt to season food. They provide astringency and dryness to balance the sweetness from accent liqueurs and syrups that give structure and weight to cocktails. A little goes a long way here. My style of bitters is what I refer to as a "longer-style bitters."

Compared with store-bought bitters, which you usually use only a couple of dashes of because they're overly astringent, these longer-style bitters allow us to incorporate additional flavor while also incorporating necessary dryness—meaning you can use more of them, thus achieving a more complex flavor without the drink being overpoweringly astringent. Most of the cocktails in this book use anywhere from ¼ to ½ oz (8 to 15 ml) of these bitters, providing an integral flavor element.

The infusions offer natural flavor accents to staple spirits, released via essential oils or maceration. These flavored syrups contribute sweetness from sugars steeped in ingredients like rosemary, chamomile, and star anise.

The importance of mouthfeel is often overlooked when preparing cocktails. But as with various accent liqueurs and fortified wines, incorporating syrups—which have a relatively thick viscosity—allows the cocktail to linger on the palate for longer, giving the olfactory system time to pick up on the delicate and defining aromatics of the other ingredients in the mixture (think spices and essential oils). You'll find that a syrup goes a long way.

This chapter's recipes are incredibly versatile. They are, of course, integral to making the drinks in this book. But I also encourage you to experiment—try adding one of the bitters, infusions, or syrups to your favorite classic cocktails, or even to creations of your very own!

BITTERS

Balsam Fir Bitters

Makes 24 oz (700 ml)

- 26 oz (750 ml) London dry gin
- 1 cup (20 g) balsam fir tips
- 2 tsp (10 g) licorice root
- 2 tsp (4 g) caraway seeds
- 2 tsp (4 g) fennel seeds
- 2 tsp (10 g) green cardamom pods
- 1 g black peppercorns

Put all the ingredients into a 68 oz (2 L) mason jar. Seal and set aside for 2 months to infuse. Using a chinois, fine-strain into another mason jar. Store at room temperature. The bitters will last indefinitely.

Cocoa Bitters

Makes 24 oz (700 ml)

- 26 oz (750 ml) rye
- 1 cup (100 g) ground cacao nibs
- 2 tsp (10 g) green cardamom pods
- 1 tsp (2 g) fennel seeds
- 5 g chopped licorice root
- One 2 × 4-inch (5 × 10 cm) cinnamon stick

Put all the ingredients into a 68-oz (2 L) mason jar. Seal and set aside for 2 months to infuse. Using a chinois, fine-strain into another mason jar. Store at room temperature. The bitters will last indefinitely.

Fennel and Chamomile Bitters

Makes 24 oz (700 ml)

- 26 oz (750 ml) gin
- 1 cup (30 g) dried chamomile flowers
- 3 g chopped licorice root
- 2 tsp (10 g) green cardamom pods
- 2 tsp (4 g) fennel seeds

Put all the ingredients into a 68 oz (2 L) mason jar. Seal and set aside for 2 months to infuse. Using a chinois, fine-strain into another mason jar. Store at room temperature. The bitters will last indefinitely.

Rosemary and Lavender Bitters

Makes 24 oz (700 ml)

- 26 oz (750 ml) London dry gin
- ¼ cup (8 g) dried lavender
- 3 tsp (6 g) fennel seeds
- 2 tsp (10 g) green cardamom pods
- 2 tsp (10 g) licorice root
- 2 g black peppercorns
- 2 vanilla beans, halved lengthwise
- 1 bunch rosemary, approximately 10 sprigs

Put all the ingredients into a 68 oz (2 L) mason jar. Seal and set aside for 2 months to infuse. Using a chinois, fine-strain into another mason jar. Store at room temperature. The bitters will last indefinitely.

Toasted Chamomile and Saffron Bitters

Makes 24 oz (700 ml)

- 26 oz (750 ml) Canadian rye
- ¾ cup (25 g) dried chamomile flowers
- 1 tbsp (6 g) caraway seeds
- 1 tbsp (6 g) fennel seeds
- 1 tbsp (15 g) green cardamom pods
- 1 tbsp (5 g) star anise pods
- 0.5 g Spanish saffron threads
- 3 vanilla beans
- One 4-inch (10 cm) cinnamon stick

In a frying pan over low heat, carefully toast the chamomile until browned and fragrant, about 15 minutes. Remove from the heat and let cool for 10 minutes. Put the toasted chamomile and all the remaining ingredients into a 68 oz (2 L) mason jar, seal, and set aside for 2 months to infuse. Using a chinois, fine-strain into another 68 oz (2 L) mason jar. Store at room temperature. The bitters will last indefinitely.

INFUSIONS

Apricot Brandy

Makes 17 oz (500 ml)

26 oz (750 ml) brandy
1 cup (150 g) dehydrated apricots

Put the brandy and apricots into a 34 oz (1 L) mason jar. Seal and set aside for 3 weeks to infuse. Using a chinois, fine-strain back into another mason jar. Store at room temperature. The infused brandy will last indefinitely.

Saffron Brandy

Makes 26 oz (750 ml)

26 oz (750 ml) brandy
1.5 g Spanish saffron threads

Put the brandy and saffron in a 34 oz (1 L) mason jar. Seal and set aside for 3 days to infuse. Using a chinois, fine-strain into another mason jar. Store at room temperature. The infused brandy will last indefinitely.

Vanilla Brandy

Makes 26 oz (750 ml)

26 oz (750 ml) brandy
4 g vanilla bean paste

Put the brandy and vanilla bean paste into a 34 oz (1 L) mason jar. Using an immersion blender, blend to incorporate. Store at room temperature. The infused brandy will last indefinitely.

Lavender Grand Marnier

Makes 26 oz (750 ml)

26 oz (750 ml) Grand Marnier
¼ cup (8 g) dried lavender

Put the Grand Marnier and lavender in a 34 oz (1 L) mason jar. Seal and set aside for 1 week to infuse. Using a chinois, fine-strain into another mason jar. Store at room temperature. The infused liqueur will last indefinitely.

Spruce Tip Gin

Makes 26 oz (750 ml)

26 oz (750 ml) London dry gin
3 g spruce tips (see note)

Put the gin and spruce tips into a 34 oz (1 L) mason jar. Seal and set aside for 2 weeks to infuse. Using a chinois, fine-strain into another mason jar. Store at room temperature. The infused gin will last indefinitely.

Note: Spruce tips can be purchased online from natural-food and health-food stores, but you can also try foraging them. (In Ontario, they are freshest at the beginning of spring.) If you are foraging, be sure to do so safely: do your research to ensure the spruce trees are not on private property and are away from roads or highly trafficked areas. Make sure to source responsibly so as not to affect the tree's growth by foraging too many. Once sourced, and rinsed, transfer to a dry kitchen towel and let dry completely in a low-light environment for approximately 2 weeks, rotating daily to ensure even drying.

Strawberry Gin

Makes 20 oz (600 ml)

26 oz (750 ml) London dry gin
9 oz (250 g) fresh strawberries, hulled and sliced

Put the gin and strawberries into a 34 oz (1 L) mason jar. Seal and set aside at room temperature for 1 week to infuse. Using a chinois, fine-strain into another mason jar. Discard the strawberries. Store at room temperature. The infused gin will last indefinitely.

Caraway Maraschino

Makes 26 oz (750 ml)

- 26 oz (750 ml) maraschino liqueur
- 11 tsp (45 g) caraway seeds

Put the maraschino and caraway into a 34 oz (1 L) mason jar. Seal and set aside for 2 weeks to infuse. Using a chinois, fine-strain and store in another mason jar. Store at room temperature. The infused liqueur will last indefinitely.

Green Cardamom Maraschino

Makes 26 oz (750 ml)

- 26 oz (750 ml) Luxardo maraschino
- 2 tbsp (25 g) green cardamom pods

Put the maraschino and cardamom into a 34 oz (1 L) mason jar. Seal and set aside for 2 weeks to infuse. Using a chinois, fine-strain into another mason jar. Store at room temperature. The infused liqueur will last indefinitely.

Lavender Maraschino

Makes 26 oz (750 ml)

- 26 oz (750 ml) Luxardo maraschino
- 6 tbsp (12 g) dried lavender

Put the maraschino and lavender into a 34 oz (1 L) mason jar. Seal and set aside for 1 week to infuse. Using a chinois, fine-strain into another mason jar. Store at room temperature. The infused liqueur will last indefinitely.

Thai Chili Maraschino

Makes 26 oz (750 ml)

- 26 oz (750 ml) Luxardo maraschino
- 5 g Thai chili, stems removed, halved lengthwise

Put the maraschino and chili into a 34 oz (1 L) mason jar. Seal and set aside for 2 days to infuse. Using a chinois, fine-strain into another mason jar. Store at room temperature. The infusion will last indefinitely.

Spiced Vodka Infusion

Makes 19 oz (550 ml)

- 26 oz (750 ml) vodka
- 6 thyme sprigs
- 3 large garlic cloves, crushed
- ½ shallot
- 1.5 g star anise pods
- 1.5 g fennel seeds
- 1.5 g caraway seeds
- 1 g black peppercorns

Put all the ingredients into a 34 oz (1 L) mason jar. Seal and set aside for 2 weeks to infuse. Using a chinois, fine-strain into another mason jar. Store at room temperature. The infusion will last indefinitely.

Cedar Rye

Makes 26 oz (750 ml)

- 26 oz (750 ml) Canadian rye
- 1¼ oz (35 g) food-grade cedarwood (see note)

Put the rye and cedar into a 34 oz (1 L) mason jar. Seal and set aside for 2 weeks to infuse. Using a chinois, fine-strain into another mason jar. Store at room temperature. The infused liquor will last indefinitely.

Note: Food-grade cedar planks can be found at kitchen supply stores, at grocery stores, and on Amazon. Carefully break one down to the required size.

SPRING

The year's first change of seasons brings the thaw of winter and the blossoming of spring. Taking a walk through the forest in the crisp air floods your senses: the soil softens beneath each step as its earthy aroma envelops you, and you can spot the fresh, vibrant leaves of new growth sprouting.

For me, when composing seasonal cocktails, spring is a season of bright, herbaceous flavors and aromatics—gin, spruce, basil, fennel seeds, cardamom—with accents of confectionary tones like violet and lavender, as well as brighter spiced notes of pastis, banana, and absinthe.

Cocktails in this chapter focus on herbaceous and brightly spice-forward compositions that represent spring and bring forth seasonal colors. For example, the color palette associated with Easter can be expressed through different flavors: lemon for yellow; fresh basil, thyme, and mint for green; grapefruit for pink; florals for violet. Spring is truly one of my favorite seasons, with corresponding flavors that pair so beautifully with its essence, drawing inspiration from fresh and vibrant florals and clean and crisp flavors.

Abstract Ice

The embodiment of abstract expressionism in the cocktail genre, this cocktail exemplifies the possibilities of flavored ice and evolving flavor profiles. This particular movement in the art world focused on challenging the conventional movement of realism, which was the style dominating the art scene in the 1940s and '50s. Inspired by Jackson Pollock's vibrant color compositions, Franz Kline's sharp, linear approach, and Mark Rothko's intention of having viewers find a personal meaning in his work, this cocktail allows guests to have a personal journey of interpretation. By deciding which of the cocktail's components to consume first, they create their own personalized composition. I found large, ornate bowls with metallic accents and varying shapes that resembled mercury with their iridescence. To me, these perfectly expressed the concept of the abstract, and, almost as if they were meant for this composition, the finished cocktail fit perfectly inside.

This cocktail is also an amazing show of the intricate way that ice can work with alcohol. Great care is needed in the proportion of ice to liquid, alcohol content, and sugar in order to create a balanced cocktail once the individual items have melted and combined. The most intriguing element of this "deconstructed" cocktail is that the flavor profile differs with each guest's interaction, depending on which components they eat first and which are left to melt into the remaining cocktail. For example, the rhubarb adds acidity, cucumber adds vegetal notes, and the black licorice adds a confectionary tone. It's a "choose your own adventure" experience and one of my favorite expressions of my individual approach to date.

Makes 1
Glass: Blown glass bowl

PLATING

- 1 tsp (5 ml) Violet and Almond Orgeat Fluid Gel (p. 28)
- 6 cilantro sprouts
- 5 tbsp (75 ml) Elderflower Snow (p. 28)
- 1 tbsp (15 ml) Black Licorice Brunoise (p. 28)
- 1 basil sprout
- 1 Cucumber Ice Bowl (p. 31)
- 1 Rhubarb Paper (p. 31)
- 1 each of Violet and Black Licorice Ice Shards (p. 28)
- ½ oz (15 ml) Lemon and Chamomile Fluid Gel (p. 73)
- 3 stems tarragon

COCKTAIL

- 1½ oz (45 ml) London dry gin
- ½ oz (15 ml) Luxardo maraschino
- 1 oz (30 ml) elderflower soda (I prefer Bottle Green)
- 2 oz (60 ml) sparkling water

To plate: In the glass bowl, starting at the 12 o'clock position and working straight down toward the center, squeeze 6 dots of the violet and almond orgeat gel to form a dotted line approximately 6 inches (15 cm) long. Place a cilantro sprout in each dot.

Place the snow in the well of the bowl, deep enough to stabilize all the ice components, approximately ½ inch (1 cm) deep. Place the brunoise on the snow at the 3 o'clock position, then place the basil sprout in the brunoise and cucumber ice bowl on top.

At the 1 o'clock position, stand the rhubarb paper upright in the snow. At the 6 o'clock position, stand the shard of violet upright. At the 9 o'clock position, stand the shard of black licorice upright.

Squeeze 6 dots of the lemon and chamomile gel on the snow, scattered around the components. Garnish 3 of the gel dots with a stem of tarragon.

To compose the cocktail: Pour the gin, maraschino, elderflower soda, and sparkling water into a pouring carafe

To serve: Pour the cocktail over the components in the glass bowl. Choose your own adventure: start with whichever edible or sippable component intrigues you.

Violet and Almond Orgeat Fluid Gel

Makes 1¾ cups (430 ml)

- 6¾ oz (200 ml) violet liqueur
- 5 oz (150 ml) water
- 1¾ oz (50 ml) almond orgeat
- 4 g agar

In a small pot over medium heat, bring the violet liqueur, water, orgeat, and agar to 198°F (92°C) for 5 seconds, to activate the agar. Transfer the mixture to a steel container and let set on a flat surface at room temperature for 1 hour, or until firm to the touch. Blend with an immersion blender until smooth. Store in a squeeze bottle in the fridge for up to 5 days.

Black Licorice Brunoise

Makes 1 cup (250 ml)

- 3½ oz (105 ml) black sambuca
- 3½ oz (105 ml) water
- 2 g agar

In a small pot over low heat, bring the sambuca, water, and agar to 195°F (91°C) and let simmer for 3 seconds, to activate the agar. Using a chinois, fine-strain into a third pan. Let set on a flat surface at room temperature until firm, approximately 45 minutes. Remove the gel from the sheet and cut into ¼-inch (6 mm) cubes. Store in an airtight container in the fridge for up to 4 days.

Elderflower Snow

Makes 2 cups (500 ml)

- 3½ oz (105 ml) St-Germain
- 1½ cups (375 ml) elderflower soda (I prefer Bottle Green)
- 2 cups (370 g) dry ice pellets (see p. 6)

In a measuring container, mix together the St-Germain and elderflower soda.

In a food processor, crush the dry ice pellets into a very fine dust, until the pieces are no larger than pea-sized, approximately 30 seconds. With the food processor on medium speed, slowly pour in the elderflower mixture. Turn off the food processor as soon as you have finished pouring. Store the snow in an airtight container in the freezer for up to 3 days.

Violet and Black Licorice Ice Shards

Makes 12 of each

- *2 oz (60 ml) steel ladle*
- 16 oz (480 ml) water
- 1¾ oz (50 ml) violet liqueur
- 2 cups (370 g) dry ice pellets (see p. 6)
- 1¾ oz (50 ml) black sambuca

In a small stainless-steel bowl, stir together 6¾ oz (200 ml) of the water and the violet liqueur.

In a food processor on medium speed, pulverize the dry ice pellets to the texture of fine sand. Fill the ladle with the dry ice to freeze the ladle. Slowly dip the ladle into the violet liqueur liquid for 1 second approximately 10 times, or until the violet ice forming on the outside of the ladle is approximately ⅓ inch (7.5 mm) thick. When dipping, leave ½ inch (1 cm) of space from the lip of the ladle and pause after each dip to allow the liquid to freeze.

Pour the dry ice in the ladle back into the food processor, then fill the ladle with warm water and let it warm until you can gently remove the violet ice bowl with your fingers. Break the ice bowl into four abstractly shaped, randomly sized shards. Repeat this process with the remaining violet liquid.

Wipe the stainless-steel bowl clean, then pour in the remaining 9¼ oz (280 ml) water and the sambuca and stir together.

Wipe the ladle clean, then fill it with dry ice. Slowly dip the ladle into the sambuca liquid and repeat the dipping process you followed for the violet ice bowls. Break the ice bowl into abstractly shaped, randomly sided shards. Repeat this process until you've used up all the sambuca liquid. Store all the shards in an airtight container in the freezer for up to 3 days.

Cucumber Ice Bowl

Makes 6

Juicer
1 oz (30 ml) steel ladle

6¾ oz (190 ml) English cucumber
2 cups (370 g) dry ice pellets (see p. 6)

Rinse the cucumber under cold running water. Cut off and discard the ends. Push the cucumber through the juicer. Using a chinois, fine-strain the juice into a measuring cup; you should have approximately 7 oz (200 ml) of juice.

In a food processor on medium speed, crush the dry ice pellets into a very fine dust, until the pieces are no larger than pea-sized, approximately 30 seconds. Fill a 1 oz (30 ml) steel ladle with the pulverized dry ice to freeze the ladle. Slowly dip the ladle into the strained cucumber juice for 1 second to coat the outside of the ladle up to ¾ inch (2 cm) from the lip, then lift the ladle out and allow the juice to freeze. Once frozen, resubmerge the ladle to create another layer of ice, level with the previous layer, until the vessel is approximately ¼ inch (6 mm) thick.

Discard the dry ice and fill the ladle with warm water. Let it warm until you can gently remove the ice bowl with your fingers. Repeat this process with the remaining cucumber juice; you should have enough to make six ice bowls. Store in the freezer for up to 3 days.

Rhubarb Paper

Makes 8 pieces

Juicer
Cheesecloth

6 stalks rhubarb
2 cups (370 g) dry ice pellets (see p. 6)

Chill a half baking sheet in the freezer for 30 minutes.

Meanwhile, gently scrub the rhubarb clean under cold running water (leaving the skin on for color). Push the rhubarb through the juicer. Using cheesecloth, fine-strain the juice into a measuring cup to remove most of the pulp; you should have approximately 1 cup (250 ml) of juice. Pour the juice into the chilled half baking sheet and freeze for 1 hour.

Break the frozen juice into abstractly shaped shards, approximately 3 × 2 inches (8 × 5 cm) each. Store in an airtight container in the freezer for up to 3 days.

Inspired Sips

Crisp, fresh flavors star here. The flavored ices from the Abstract Ice work beautifully in these—the cucumber is a seamless pairing.

Cardamom Spritz

Makes 1 • Glass: White wine

3 oz (90 ml) Champagne
¾ oz (23 ml) St-Germain
¼ oz (8 ml) Green Cardamom Maraschino (p. 19)
¼ oz (8 ml) Balsam Fir Bitters (p. 16)
1 sugar cube
Celery string, to garnish
Grapefruit peel, to garnish

Put the Champagne, St-Germain, maraschino, bitters, and sugar cube into a mixing glass. Fill the mixing glass with ice and stir to chill, approximately three rotations. Using a Hawthorne strainer, strain into a stemless white wine glass. Using a peeler, peel a thin slice of celery and place on ice cubes. Gently squeeze the peel between your index finger and thumb to extract the oils into the cocktail. Discard the peel. Serve.

Tokyo and Thyme

Makes 1 • Glass: Coupe

1 oz (30 ml) nigori sake
1 oz (30 ml) coconut rum
¾ oz (23 ml) fresh lemon juice
½ oz (15 ml) Thyme Syrup (p. 21)
¼ oz (8 ml) Green Cardamom Maraschino (p. 19)
1 egg white
Edible flower petals, to garnish
Grapefruit peel, to garnish

Put the sake, rum, lemon juice, syrup, maraschino, and egg white into a shaker. Dry shake for 5 seconds to aerate the egg white. Fill the shaker with ice and shake for 2 seconds to chill. Using a Hawthorne strainer, fine-strain into a coupe glass. Float the edible flower petals on top. Gently squeeze the peel between your index finger and thumb to extract the oils into the cocktail. Discard the peel. Serve.

Mezcal Spring Days

Makes 1 • Glass: Coupe

1 ¼ oz (38 ml) mezcal
¼ oz (8 ml) St-Germain
¼ oz (8 ml) Lillet Blanc
¼ oz (8 ml) Green Cardamom Maraschino (p. 19)
⅙ oz (5 ml) pastis
4 slices cucumber
Dill flowers, to garnish
Grapefruit peel, to garnish

Put the mezcal, St-Germain, Lillet Blanc, maraschino, pastis, and cucumber into a mixing glass. Muddle the cucumber slices to extract their flavor. Fill the mixing glass with ice and stir to chill, approximately three rotations. Using a Hawthorne strainer and fine cocktail strainer, strain into a coupe glass. Garnish with the dill flowers. Gently squeeze the peel between your index finger and thumb to extract the oils into the cocktail. Discard the peel. Serve.

Pictured opposite: Cardamom Spritz

Spring Thaw

This cocktail perfectly encapsulates the thaw of winter and the blossoming of spring. The live sheet moss dressing this cocktail mixes with the notes of cedar, lilac, grapefruit, and soil to evoke the fresh lilacs that bloom in Ontario's rustic forests. When I served this to one BarChef guest, the aroma alone evoked gentle tears, and they shared with me their memories of playing in their grandma's backyard. Being able to ignite this kind of experience for guests as they're transported to a nostalgic time is one of the main motivations behind all my modernist compositions. I try to find new ways to evoke this, like pouring the chamomile-tinged drink overtop Campari and a vanilla ice sphere to release the unripe strawberry and floral tones within.

Makes 1
Glass: Stemless goblet

PLATING

- 4 × 2-feet (122 × 60 cm) piece chicken wire
- 8 × 8 × 3-inch (20 × 20 × 8 cm) ceramic bento box
- Live sheet moss
- 10 stems live greens (I prefer myrtle, juniper, or cedar)
- 8 stems wax flowers
- 6 goldenrods (or other yellow flower)
- 6 snapdragons
- 4 pussy willows

- 2 tbsp (30 ml) Spring Thaw Aroma (p. 36)
- 1 cup (185 g) dry ice pellets (see p. 6)
- Red Grapefruit, Orange Blossom, and Vanilla Air (p. 36)
- 1 Campari and Vanilla Granita Sphere (p. 36)
- 5 edible flower petals
- 3 micro basil sprouts

COCKTAIL

Serving carafe

- 3 oz (90 ml) sparkling wine
- 1½ oz (45 ml) Bombay Sapphire gin
- 1½ oz (45 ml) Chamomile Syrup (p. 20)
- 1 Campari and Vanilla Granita Sphere (p. 36)

To plate: Arrange the molded chicken wire in the bento box to form a 3-inch (8 cm) diameter tube, to stabilize the greens and floral stems. Pour in the spring thaw aroma. Cover the chicken wire with the sheet moss. Place the goblet at the front and center of the box. Set aside.

Trim the stems of the greens, wax flowers, goldenrods, snapdragons, and pussy willows; keep most between 12 and 14 inches (30 and 35 cm) but some a bit shorter. Arrange the greens and floral to resemble a garden by sticking the stems through the sheet moss to stand upright in the chicken wire, placing the shortest pieces at the front of the bento box (framing the goblet), with the next tallest stems in the row behind. Repeat until the box is filled.

Carefully lift the service piece and place the dry ice pellets underneath the moss in the bento box, ensuring no dry ice or chicken wire is visible.

Boil a kettle of water.

Put 3 tbsp (45 ml) of air into the goblet. Place the sphere on top, and garnish with the edible flower petals and micro basil sprouts.

To compose the cocktail: Pour all the cocktail ingredients into a carafe.

To serve: Pour the cocktail from the carafe into the goblet overtop the sphere and air. Pour the boiling water over the moss to activate the dry ice and aromatics beneath. Serve.

Spring Thaw Aroma

Makes 3½ tbsp (55 ml)

- 3 tbsp (45 ml) organic food-grade Virginia cedar essential oil
- 1 tsp (5 ml) organic food-grade red grapefruit essential oil
- ¼ tsp (1 ml) perfume lilac oil

Pour all the ingredients into an airtight glass bottle. Store at room temperature for up to 2 weeks.

Campari and Vanilla Granita Spheres

Makes 3

Three 2½-inch (6 cm) spherical ice molds

- 1½ cups (375 ml) water
- 2 oz (60 ml) Campari
- 2 oz (60 ml) Vanilla Syrup (p. 21)

In a measuring container, combine the water, Campari, and vanilla syrup. Pour into the molds (the syrup should fill three molds). Freeze until frozen, approximately 4 hours. Store in the freezer for up to 1 week.

Red Grapefruit, Orange Blossom, and Vanilla Air

Makes approximately 4 cups (1 L)

- 4 cups (1 L) water
- 1 cup (250 ml) Vanilla Syrup (p. 21)
- 1 oz (30 ml) orange blossom water
- 1 drop organic food-grade red grapefruit essential oil
- 4 g soy lecithin

Prepare this air immediately before composing the cocktail. Put the water, vanilla syrup, orange blossom water, essential oil, and lecithin into a deep plastic bowl. Using an immersion blender, blend until the lecithin is dissolved, then blend the surface area of the mixture to form foam. Let set for 1 minute, then use immediately.

Inspired Sips

Spring breaks through with bright, floral tones, touched by herbaceous elements and dark, caramelized notes.

Agave Nature

Makes 1 • Glass: Wine

1 ½ oz (45 ml) reposado tequila
½ oz (15 ml) Chamomile Syrup (p. 20)
¼ oz (8 ml) Campari
¼ oz (8 ml) Madeira
⅛ oz (4 ml) pastis
Orange peel, to garnish

Put the tequila, syrup, Campari, Madeira, and pastis into a mixing glass with ice. Stir to chill, approximately three rotations. Using a fine cocktail strainer, strain into a wine glass. Gently squeeze the peel between your index finger and thumb to extract the oils into the cocktail. Discard the peel. Serve.

Moroccan Old-Fashioned

Makes 1 • Glass: Double old-fashioned

1 oz (30 ml) bourbon
¼ oz (8 ml) Saffron Brandy (p. 18)
¼ oz (8 ml) Chamomile Syrup (p. 20)
¼ oz (8 ml) Cocoa Bitters (p. 16)
3 peels orange

Put all the ingredients except for 1 orange peel into a double old-fashioned glass. Muddle the 2 orange peels. Fill the glass with ice and stir to chill, approximately three rotations. Garnish the cocktail with a flamed orange peel: Hold a lit match beside the cocktail in one hand and the remaining orange peel in the other. Squeeze the peel between your index finger and thumb toward the match, igniting the oils from the peel. Discard the peel. Serve.

El Mariachi

Makes 1 • Glass: Double old-fashioned

1 ½ oz (45 ml) mezcal
½ oz (15 ml) Chamomile Syrup (p. 20)
½ oz (15 ml) Balsam Fir Bitters (p. 16)
¼ oz (8 ml) Luxardo maraschino
¼ oz (8 ml) Lillet Blanc
3 peels red grapefruit
Mint crown, to garnish

Pour the mezcal, syrup, bitters, maraschino, and Lillet Blanc into a double old-fashioned glass. Add 2 grapefruit peels and muddle. Fill the glass with ice and stir to chill, approximately three rotations. Gently squeeze the remaining peel between your index finger and thumb to extract the oils into the cocktail. Discard the peel. Garnish with fresh mint. Serve.

Pictured opposite: Moroccan Old-Fashioned

Elderflowers and Fougère

The French word *fougère*, which directly translates to "fern," is used in the perfume industry as an olfactive descriptor for scents that are fresh, clean, and green. These evocative elements were the inspiration behind the crisp flavor profile of this cocktail. Then, to capture the pure essence of fougère, I incorporated green ingredients that would evoke this flavor profile—think cucumber, mint, basil, dill, Chartreuse, green grass. Along with live fern leaves that create an immersive canopy of green, the black earth's color and texture further accentuate the natural elements through flavor and aroma.

Makes 1
Glass: Round footed glass terrarium

PLATING

- Four 6 × 4 × 3-inch (15 × 10 × 8 cm) pieces of floral foam
- 14-inch (35 cm) diameter, 3-inch (8 cm) high glass bowl
- 2 round glass terrariums (1 large, 1 small)
- 6 cups (1.5 L) black earth
- 3 fern leaves (helecho or leather ferns)
- Coaster

- 5 tbsp (75 ml) Green Grass and Elderflower Snow (p. 42)
- 3 tbsp (45 ml) Green Grass Air (p. 43)
- 3 Cucumber Ice Shards (p. 42)
- 1 large mint sprig
- 1 tbsp (15 ml) Mint and Chartreuse Fluid Gel (p. 43) + more to garnish
- 4 dill flowers
- 4 micro basil sprouts
- 1 tbsp (15 ml) Spruce and Chartreuse Chantilly (p. 42)
- 8 cups (2 L) liquid nitrogen
- Zest from ⅛ lime

COCKTAIL

- 4 oz (120 ml) elderflower soda
- ½ oz (15 ml) Thyme Syrup (p. 21)
- ½ oz (15 ml) Spruce Tip Gin (p. 18)
- ¼ oz (8 ml) mezcal
- ¼ oz (8 ml) Green Cardamom Maraschino (p. 19)
- ⅙ oz (5 ml) green Chartreuse

To plate: Trim the edges of the floral foam to neatly fit into the glass service piece. Cut out an area for the small terrarium to sit in, then place the terrarium in the foam, allowing it to be partly hidden with the foam.

Fill the glass service piece with black earth. Stand the fern leaves at the back of the service piece to create a background for the composition. Place a coaster on top of the earth on the left side of the bowl, then place the large terrarium on the coaster.

In the center of the large terrarium, put 3 tbsp (45 ml) snow. Place the green grass air on top of the snow at the back of the glass. Stand up the cucumber ice shards in the snow, then place the mint among the shards.

In the small terrarium, put the remaining 2 tbsp (30 ml) snow. Garnish the snow with 6 randomly placed dots of mint and Chartreuse gel. Stick the dill flowers and basil into alternating dots of gel.

Carefully put the spruce and Chartreuse Chantilly into the liquid nitrogen for 30 seconds to poach, dusting with lime zest (this accentuates the Chantilly's aromatics and flavor while in the nitrogen).

To compose the cocktail: Fill a mixing glass with ice. Pour in all the cocktail ingredients and stir to chill, approximately three rotations. Using a cocktail strainer, fine-strain into a glass carafe.

Place the poached Chantilly among the fluid gel dots in the center of the terrarium.

To serve: Pour the cocktail into the larger terrarium, over the snow and ice components, allowing all the ingredients to mix for the finished cocktail. Serve.

Green Grass and Elderflower Snow

Makes approximately 2 cups (500 ml)

- 1 oz (28 g) freshly cut wheatgrass
- 2 cups (500 ml) elderflower soda
- 2 cups (370 g) dry ice pellets (see p. 6)

In a measuring cup, use an immersion blender to blend the grass and elderflower soda until the grass is smoothly and evenly distributed. Using a chinois, fine-strain into a measuring cup.

In a food processor, crush the dry ice pellets into a very fine dust, until the pieces are no larger than pea-sized, approximately 30 seconds. With the food processor on medium speed, slowly pour in the elderflower mixture. Turn off the food processor as soon as you have finished pouring. Store the snow in an airtight container in the freezer for up to 6 days.

Spruce and Chartreuse Chantilly

Makes approximately 2 cups (500 ml)

iSi siphon and charger (see p. 8)

- 1 cup (250 ml) 35% whipping cream
- 3½ oz (105 ml) Spruce Tip Gin (p. 18)
- ¼ cup (50 g) white sugar
- 2 oz (55 ml) green Chartreuse
- 1 sheet gelatin

Prepare an ice bath.

Prepare a double boiler: Place a stainless-steel bowl atop a pot filled about halfway with water set over medium heat (the bowl should be the same circumference as the pan). Place all the ingredients in the bowl and stir slowly until the gelatin is fully melted.

Transfer the gelatin to the iSi siphon, close, and shake vigorously for 1 minute, then charge with the nitrous oxide charger. Put the siphon in the ice bath and chill for 1 hour. Store the siphon in the fridge for up to 5 days.

Cucumber Ice Shards

Makes approximately 25

- 4 to 5 English cucumbers
- Pulverized dry ice

In a juicer, juice 4 cucumbers. Using a chinois, fine-strain into a measuring cup. You should have 3 cups (700 ml) of cucumber juice; juice another cucumber if you need to.

Into a half baking sheet set on a flat surface, slowly pour the cucumber juice to the depth of ½ inch (1 cm). Carefully dust with the pulverized dry ice to freeze, doing so very slowly to avoid bubbling. Once the juice is fully frozen, use an offset spatula to break the ice into shards that will fit inside the cocktail terrarium, approximately 3 × 2 inches (8 × 5 cm) each. Store in an airtight container in the freezer for up to 3 days.

Mint and Chartreuse Fluid Gel

Makes approximately 2 cups (500 ml)

- 9 cups (2.25 L) water
- 1½ oz (43 g) mint leaves (approximately 40)
- 5 oz (150 ml) Mint Syrup (p. 20)
- 3¼ oz (98 ml) green Chartreuse
- ¼ oz (7 g) agar

Prepare an ice bath.

In a medium pot over high heat, bring 8 cups (2 L) of water to a boil. Add the mint leaves and boil for 3 minutes, using tongs to make sure the mint is constantly submerged. Using the tongs, quickly transfer the mint to a chinois to drain. Submerge the mint in the chinois in the ice bath, agitating until the mint leaves are cold to the touch. Set aside in the ice bath.

In a medium pot over medium heat, bring the remaining 1 cup (250 ml) water, the mint syrup, green Chartreuse, and agar to 195°F (91°C) and let simmer for 3 seconds to activate the agar, then quickly pour the mixture into a measuring cup. Add the drained blanched mint. Using an immersion blender, blend the mixture until smooth and dark green.

Using a chinois, quickly fine-strain the mixture into a steel bowl and place in the fridge to let set fully (it should be firm to the touch), approximately 30 minutes. Transfer to a quarter pan and use an immersion blender to blend the mixture until smooth. Store in a squeeze bottle in the fridge for up to 3 days. Discard once it begins to brown.

Green Grass Air

Makes approximately 4 cups (1 L)

- ¾ oz (21 g) freshly cut wheatgrass
- 4 cups (1 L) water
- 2 g soy lecithin

In a measuring cup, use an immersion blender to blend the grass and 1 cup (250 ml) water until fully incorporated. Add the remaining 3 cups (750 ml) water and blend to thoroughly mix. Using a chinois, fine-strain into a deep plastic bowl.

Add the lecithin. Hold the immersion blender to the surface of the mixture and blend to create foam. Let sit for 10 seconds. Store in an airtight container in the fridge for up to 1 day.

Inspired Sips

Elderflowers and Fougère's green elements are intriguingly twisted with coconut, chili, and licorice.

Rose Gold Margarita

Makes 1 • Glass: Coupe

- 1½ oz (45 ml) Thyme Syrup (p. 21)
- 1 tsp (6 g) pink Himalayan salt
- 1½ oz (45 ml) reposado tequila
- ¾ oz (23 ml) fresh lime juice
- ¼ oz (8 ml) Thai Chili Maraschino (p. 19)
- ¼ oz (8 ml) Campari

Dip the rim of a coupe glass in ¾ oz (23 ml) thyme syrup, then in the Himalayan salt, being careful to apply a thin line of salt on the glass. In a shaker, pour in the remaining ¾ oz (23 ml) thyme syrup, the tequila, lime juice, Thai chili maraschino, and Campari. Fill the shaker with ice and shake for 5 seconds to chill. Using a fine cocktail strainer, strain into the coupe glass. Serve.

Coconut and Cardamom Spritz

Makes 1 • Glass: Highball

- 1 oz (30 ml) coconut rum
- ½ oz (15 ml) Green Cardamom Maraschino (p. 19)
- ½ oz (15 ml) St-Germain
- ½ oz (15 ml) Thyme Syrup (p. 21)
- ⅙ oz (5 ml) pastis
- 2 cucumber coins
- 3 oz (90 ml) soda water
- 2 tbsp (30 ml) Green Grass Air (p. 43)
- Thin slice of grapefruit peel

Pour the rum, maraschino, St-Germain, syrup, and pastis in a highball glass. Fill the glass with ice. Garnish with the cucumbers and top with soda water. Then top with the green grass air. Gently squeeze the peel between your index finger and thumb to extract the oils into the cocktail. Discard the peel. Serve.

Coconut and Absinthe Sour

Makes 1 • Glass: Coupe

- 1½ oz (45 ml) coconut rum
- ¼ oz (8 ml) absinthe
- 1 oz (30 ml) pineapple juice
- ¾ oz (23 ml) fresh lemon juice
- ¾ oz (23 ml) Vanilla Syrup (p. 21)
- 1 egg white
- Thin slice of grapefruit peel
- Edible flower petals (I like yellow marigolds)

Put the rum, absinthe, juices, syrup, and egg white into a shaker and dry shake to aerate the egg white. Fill the shaker with ice and shake for 5 seconds to chill. Using a fine cocktail strainer, strain into a coupe glass. Gently squeeze the peel between your index finger and thumb to extract the oils into the cocktail. Discard the peel. Top the cocktail with edible flower petals, placing them in the center. Serve.

Pictured opposite: Coconut and Absinthe Sour

Geometric Lavender

Makes 1
Glass: Footed ceramic bowl

PLATING

Medium shallow bowl
Medium glass cloche
One 4-inch (10 cm) diameter steel cannoli tube

2 cups (64 g) dried lavender (enough to fill the bowl)
12 Aperol Geometric Cream Gels (p. 49)
12 Violet Geometric Cream Gels (p. 49)
12 Cardamom Geometric Cream Gels (p. 49)
1 White Chocolate and Pastis Demisphere (p. 50)
6 micro basil sprouts
3 tbsp (45 ml) Aperol and Lavender Pearls (p. 51)
2 tbsp (30 ml) Violet Fluid Gel (p. 63)
2 cups (500 ml) White Chocolate and Lavender Snow (p. 51)
1 Violet Cream and Lavender Nitro Coil (p. 50)
3 tbsp (45 ml) Red Grapefruit Cells (p. 51)

COCKTAIL

Serving carafe

1½ oz (45 ml) London dry gin
1 oz (30 ml) soda water
¼ oz (8 ml) Thyme Syrup (p. 21)
⅛ oz (4 ml) Green Cardamom Maraschino (p. 19)
⅛ oz (4 ml) Lavender Maraschino (p. 19)
1⁄16 oz (1.5 ml) pastis

For this cocktail, I was inspired by lavender farms in southern France, where the flower's naturally sporadic growth is seemingly confined within the field's straight geometric lines. Still, it escapes these geometric limitations by the way its amazing aroma overwhelms the area around it. With this cocktail, the lavender isn't contained for long: the geometric enclosure of the cloche is soon removed to release the lavender aromatics tableside. Along with the floral and citrus, the other geometry at play here—a honeycomb's hexagon, the spiral of a beehive—is a nod to a bee's role in pollination, which is an integral element of natural evolution, growth, and beauty.

To plate: Place the lavender in a shallow bowl. Set aside.

In the footed ceramic bowl, starting at the 9 o'clock position and working clockwise until you reach 12 o'clock, alternate placing 2 Aperol geometric cream gel cells, then 2 violet cells, then 2 cardamom cells until you have used all the gel cells to create a honeycomb shape.

Place the demisphere at the 5 o'clock position. Garnish the demisphere with 1 basil sprout, then garnish 2 of the cardamom gel cells with 1 basil sprout each.

Arrange the pearls at the 7 o'clock position, and garnish with dots of the violet gel.

Place the snow in the center of the bowl. Top with the coil, then garnish with 3 dots of the violet gel and the remaining 3 basil sprouts.

At the 3 o'clock position, place the red grapefruit cells.

Settle the footed bowl in the lavender. Put the cloche overtop.

To compose the cocktail: Pour all the cocktail ingredients into the serving carafe.

To serve: For the best aromatic effect, serve the cocktail at the table by removing the cloche and pouring the cocktail from the serving carafe over the plated components.

Aperol, Violet, and Cardamom Geometric Cream Gels

Makes approximately 72 gel cells total (24 of each flavor)

Thirty-six ½-inch (1 cm) diameter hexagon silicone molds

5 oz (150 ml) Aperol
6¾ oz (200 ml) 10% cream
¼ oz (7 g) agar
5 oz (150 ml) violet liqueur
5 oz (150 ml) Green Cardamom Maraschino (p. 19)
1¾ oz (50 ml) water

In a small pot over medium heat, bring the Aperol, 1¾ oz (50 ml) cream, and 2 g agar to 200°F (93°C) and let simmer for 3 seconds, to activate the agar. Pour into 12 of the hexagon molds and let set on a flat surface at room temperature, about 45 minutes.

Wipe the pot clean and, over medium heat, bring the violet liqueur, 1¾ oz (50 ml) cream, and 2 g agar to 195°F (91°C) and let simmer for 3 seconds, to activate the agar. Pour into 12 of the molds and let set on a flat surface at room temperature, about 45 minutes.

Wipe the pot clean again and, over medium heat, bring the green cardamom maraschino, 3¼ oz (98 ml) cream, water, and 3 g agar to 195°F (91°C) for 3 seconds. Pour into 12 of the molds and let set on a flat surface at room temperature, about 45 minutes.

Remove the gels from their molds and cut each in half lengthwise. Store in a parchment paper–lined airtight container in the fridge for up to 1 week.

White Chocolate Water

Makes approximately 2 cups (500 ml)

2 cups (500 ml) water
2½ oz (75 g) Baker's white chocolate

In a medium pot over low heat, heat the water and white chocolate until the chocolate has melted, stirring with a wooden spoon to avoid burning. Transfer to a steel container and cover with plastic wrap. Using a fork, poke holes into the wrap. Refrigerate the mixture overnight, or until a solid white layer of fat forms on the surface.

Using a chinois, fine-strain the chocolate water into an airtight container. Store in the fridge for up to 1 week. Keep it covered to prevent the liquid from absorbing odors from the fridge. (Feel free to freeze any extra white chocolate water in ice cube molds, to chill your favorite gin-based cocktail at home—try with a Negroni for a delicious confectionary twist on the classic.)

Violet Cream and Lavender Nitro Coils

Makes approximately 10

One 6-foot (1.8 m) clear food-grade rubber tube
Large plastic syringe
iSi siphon and charger (see p. 8)
¾-inch (2 cm) steel cannoli tube

4¼ oz (125 ml) violet liqueur
3¼ oz (98 ml) 10% cream
1 oz (30 ml) Lavender Maraschino (p. 19)
2.5 g agar
2 g gellan gum
8 cups (2 L) liquid nitrogen

Prepare a large ice bath.

Put the violet liqueur, cream, lavender maraschino, agar, and gellan gum in a measuring container and, using an immersion blender, blend until thoroughly mixed. Transfer to a medium pot and, over medium heat, bring the mixture to 195°F (91°C) and let simmer for 3 seconds, to activate the agar.

Place one end of the tube in the coil mixture. Holding the syringe at the other end, create a suction to draw the mixture into the tube. Transfer the tube to the ice bath and fully submerge. Let the mixture set for 30 minutes, then remove the tube from the ice bath and set aside.

Charge an iSi siphon with nitrous oxide. Stick the nozzle into the mixture in the tube and gently press the trigger to extract the "noodle" into a bowl. Using your hands, carefully wrap the noodle around the cannoli tube. Using tongs, carefully submerge in liquid nitrogen for 10 seconds, until frozen. Using the tongs, carefully remove the coil and let warm slightly to avoid cracking at the next step. Pour warm water inside the cannoli tube to loosen and remove the coil. Store in an airtight container in the freezer for up to 1 week. (You can use extras for garnishing, such as for the Spruce Ramos Fizz, page 52.)

White Chocolate and Pastis Demispheres

Makes approximately 20 demispheres or 10 full spheres

Twenty 1-inch (2.5 cm) demisphere molds

2½ oz (75 g) Baker's white chocolate
2½ oz (75 ml) Pernod pastis
3.5 g agar
5 oz (150 ml) 10% cream
5 oz (150 ml) water

In a container and using an immersion blender, blend all the ingredients until smooth. Transfer to a medium pot and place over medium heat, stirring until the chocolate melts and being careful not to burn it. Bring the mixture to 200°F (93°C) and let simmer for just 5 seconds, to activate the agar. Pour into the demisphere molds and let set on a flat surface at room temperature, approximately 45 minutes. Store in a parchment paper–lined airtight container in the fridge for up to 3 days.

Aperol and Lavender Pearls

Makes approximately 50

Steel strainer

6¾ oz (200 ml) Aperol

3¼ oz (98 ml) Lavender Maraschino (p. 19)

3¼ oz (98 ml) water

¼ oz (7 g) agar

1 g xanthan gum

8 cups (2 L) liquid nitrogen

In a medium pot over medium heat and using an immersion blender, blend the Aperol, maraschino, water, agar, and xanthan gum until fully incorporated, bringing the mixture to 201°F (94°C) and let simmer for 3 seconds, to activate the agar. Transfer to a squeeze bottle while the mixture is still warm, to avoid setting.

Submerge a steel strainer in liquid nitrogen and slowly squeeze the bottle of Aperol mixture into the strainer to create pea-sized pearls. Leave to set in the liquid nitrogen for 15 minutes. Transfer to an airtight container and freeze to temper, 30 minutes. Store in the freezer for up to 3 days.

White Chocolate and Lavender Snow

Makes approximately 2 cups (500 ml)

1½ cups (375 ml) White Chocolate Water (p. 49)

1 oz (30 ml) Lavender Maraschino (p. 19)

2 cups (370 g) dry ice pellets (see p. 6)

In a measuring container, combine the white chocolate water and lavender maraschino.

In a food processor, crush the dry ice pellets into a very fine dust, until the pieces are no larger than pea-sized, approximately 30 seconds. With the food processor on medium speed, slowly pour in the chocolate mixture. Turn off the food processor as soon as you have finished pouring. Store the snow in an airtight container in the freezer for up to 3 days.

Red Grapefruit Cells

Makes 5 tbsp (75 ml)

Steel strainer

1 red grapefruit

8 cups (2 L) liquid nitrogen

Carefully peel the grapefruit, removing as much pith as possible. Using a paring knife, carefully segment the grapefruit, ensuring there is no pith attached.

Place a steel strainer in a bath of liquid nitrogen for 3 seconds, then place the segments in the strainer for 15 seconds, until frosted and frozen. (A steel strainer is critical here, since it is being submerged in the liquid nitrogen.) Wrapping a cloth around the handle of the strainer, carefully remove the strainer from the bath and, using a spoon, transfer the segments to a mortar.

The segments will have frozen together, so, using a pestle, gently break them apart into individual cells. Transfer to an airtight container and freeze for 30 minutes to temper. Store in the freezer for up to 3 days.

Inspired Sips

Geometric Lavender's floral-citrus fields lead to these spruce-forward sips.

Spruce Ramos Fizz

Makes 1 • Glass: Collins

1 oz (30 ml) Spruce Tip Gin (p. 18)
1 oz (30 ml) 35% heavy cream
1 oz (30 ml) Thyme Syrup (p. 21)
¾ oz (23 ml) fresh lemon juice
¼ oz (8 ml) Green Cardamom Maraschino (p. 19)
1 egg white
2 oz (60 ml) soda water, as cold as possible
¾ oz (23 ml) Aperol
Juniper sprig, to garnish
Violet Cream and Lavender Nitro Coil, to garnish (p. 50, optional)
Red grapefruit peel, to garnish

Put the gin, cream, syrup, lemon juice, maraschino, and egg white into a shaker. Shake for 5 seconds to aerate the egg white. Fill the shaker with ice and shake for 5 seconds to chill. Pour the soda water into a collins glass. Using a cocktail strainer, fine-strain the gin mixture into the glass. Slowly pour the Aperol into cocktail to create a layered effect. Garnish with the juniper and the nitro coil (if using). Gently squeeze the peel between your index finger and thumb to extract the oils into the cocktail. Discard the peel. Serve.

Ice Wine and Aperol Spritz

Makes 1 • Glass: Wine

1½ oz (45 ml) late harvest Vidal
¾ oz (23 ml) Thyme Syrup (p. 21)
¼ oz (8 ml) Aperol
⅛ oz (4 ml) pastis
1 oz (30 ml) soda water
Mint sprig, to garnish
Red grapefruit peel, to garnish

Pour the Vidal, syrup, Aperol, and pastis into a wine glass and stir. Add 4 ice cubes and the soda. Garnish with the mint. Gently squeeze the peel between your index finger and thumb to extract the oils into the cocktail. Discard the peel. Serve.

Spruce Frost

Makes 1 • Glass: Coupe

1½ oz (45 ml) Spruce Tip Gin (p. 18)
¾ oz (23 ml) Rosemary Syrup (p. 21)
¼ oz (8 ml) Caraway Maraschino (p. 19)
¼ oz (8 ml) green Chartreuse
1 egg white
1 piece cacao nib, to garnish

Put the gin, syrup, maraschino, Chartreuse, and egg white into a shaker and dry shake for 5 seconds to emulsify and aerate the ingredients. Fill the shaker with ice and shake for 2 seconds to chill. Strain into a coupe glass. Grate the cacao nib overtop to garnish. Serve.

Pictured opposite: Spruce Ramos Fizz

Night Blossom

This cocktail is a celebration of the art of abstract, with touches of surrealism and contemporary, the presentation reminiscent of a Salvador Dali composition with its flow of color, flavor, and aroma. It was inspired by a late-night stroll in a local park after an evening shift, and walking by a tree that was illuminated by a nearby streetlamp, with the visual accents of early blooming greens and florals. The Night Blossom was an integral cocktail on the BarChef program in 2014 because of the use of liquid nitrogen. This led to the execution of the noodle component in this cocktail, which was only the start: we continued to find various applications for liquid nitrogen as the modernist cocktail movement progressed, opening the flood gates of creativity.

Makes 1
Glass: Ramen bowl

COCKTAIL

Ceramic serving carafe

1½ oz (45 ml) bourbon
1½ oz (45 ml) almond orgeat
½ oz (15 ml) Luxardo maraschino
⅓ oz (10 ml) Islay Scotch
¼ oz (8 ml) Rosemary Syrup (p. 21)

PLATING

Chopsticks
12 oz (350 ml) steel ladle

5 tbsp (75 ml) Almond Orgeat and Maple Snow (p. 56)
1 Balsam Fir and Honey Julienne (p. 56)
1 Violet Julienne (p. 56)
2 Patchouli and Amaro Marbles (p. 57)
8 cups (2 L) liquid nitrogen
1 Cacao and Chartreuse Branch (p. 57)
1 tbsp (15 ml) Violet and Almond Orgeat Fluid Gel (p. 28)
1 tbsp (15 ml) Mint and Chartreuse Fluid Gel (p. 43)
Mint sprig, to garnish

To compose the cocktail: Pour all the cocktail ingredients into a shaker filled with ice. Shake for 2 seconds to chill. Using a Hawthorne strainer, strain the cocktail into the ceramic serving carafe.

To plate: Put the snow into a ramen bowl. Top with the balsam fir and honey julienne and the violet julienne. Add the marbles.

Fill the bowl of the ladle with the liquid nitrogen. Place the cacao branch in the ladle and carefully lower into the liquid nitrogen bath, leaving the branch in it for 10 seconds. Using silicone tongs, remove the branch and place in the center of the ramen bowl on top of the snow.

Create "leaves" on the branch with 5 dots of the violet and orgeat gel and 5 dots of the mint and Chartreuse gel. Lastly, place the mint in the snow.

To serve: Pour the prepared cocktail over the branch and snow components in the bowl.

Almond Orgeat and Maple Snow

Makes approximately 2 cups (500 ml)

¾ cup (180 ml) water
⅔ cup (150 ml) almond orgeat
5 tbsp (75 ml) maple syrup
2 cups (370 g) dry ice pellets (see p. 6)

Pour the water, almond orgeat, and maple syrup into a measuring container.

In a food processor, crush the dry ice pellets into a very fine dust, until the pieces are no larger than pea-sized, approximately 30 seconds. With the food processor on medium speed, slowly pour in the almond-maple mixture. Turn off the food processor as soon as you have finished pouring. Store the snow in an airtight container in the freezer for up to 3 days.

Balsam Fir and Honey Juliennes

Makes approximately 10

4¼ oz (125 ml) water
1¾ oz (50 ml) Balsam Fir Bitters (p. 16)
¾ oz (23 ml) honey
2 g agar

In a small pot over medium heat, bring the water, balsam fir bitters, honey, and agar to 203°F (95°C) and let simmer for just 5 seconds, to activate the agar. Transfer to a rectangular plastic container and let set on a flat surface at room temperature, approximately 45 minutes. Invert the container and, using your hands, carefully remove the set gel. Square up any rounded corners, then julienne the gel into strips ¼ inch (6 mm) wide. Store in an airtight container in the fridge for up to 3 days.

Violet Juliennes

Makes approximately 10

3½ oz (105 ml) violet liqueur
3½ oz (105 ml) water
2 g agar

In a small pot over medium heat, bring the violet liqueur, water, and agar to 203°F (95°C) and let simmer for just 5 seconds, to activate the agar. Transfer to a rectangular plastic container and let set on a flat surface at room temperature, approximately 45 minutes. Invert the container and, using your hands, carefully remove the set gel. Square up any rounded corners, then julienne the gel into strips ¼ inch (6 mm) wide. Store the juliennes in an airtight container in the fridge for up to 3 days.

Cacao and Chartreuse Branch

Makes approximately 5

One 6-foot (15 cm) clear food-grade rubber tube
Large plastic syringe
iSi siphon and charger (see p. 8)

10 oz (300 ml) 10% cream
1 oz (28 g) Baker's unsweetened chocolate
3½ oz (105 ml) water
3½ oz (105 ml) green Chartreuse
2 tbsp (24 g) white sugar
3.5 g agar
3 g gellan gum

Prepare an ice bath.

In a small pot over medium heat, heat the cream, chocolate, water, green Chartreuse, sugar, agar, and gellan gum, stirring constantly until everything is melted. Bring the mixture to 195°F (91°C) and let simmer for just 5 seconds, to activate the agar, then turn off the heat.

Place one end of the plastic tube in the branch mixture. Holding the syringe at the other end, create a suction to draw the mixture into the tube. Place the tube in the ice bath for 5 minutes to set, then remove and set aside. Charge an iSi siphon with nitrous oxide. Stick the nozzle into the mixture in the tube and gently press the trigger to expel the "branch" into an airtight plastic container. Store in the fridge for up to 3 days.

Patchouli and Amaro Marbles

Makes approximately 100

10 cups (2.5 L) + 5¼ oz (158 ml) water
+ more for water rinse bath
½ oz (14 g) sodium alginate
1 cup + 1 tsp (255 ml) Patchouli Syrup (p. 21)
1¾ oz (50 ml) Amaro Lucano
4 g calcium lactate gluconate
0.6 g xanthan gum

In a plastic container and using an immersion blender, blend 10 cups of water with the sodium alginate, until the sodium alginate is fully dissolved. Let sit until all the air bubbles have dissipated.

Prepare a water rinse bath in a clear plastic bowl.

Prepare a patchouli bath by blending ⅔ cup (150 ml) patchouli syrup and 3½ oz (105 ml) water in an airtight container.

Put the remaining 3½ oz (105 ml) patchouli syrup, the Amaro Lucano, calcium lactate gluconate, and 1¾ oz (50 ml) water into a measuring container. Using an immersion blender, blend until fully dissolved. Skim the surface with a spoon to remove any air bubbles. Add the xanthan gum and blend again until dissolved. Transfer to an airtight container and let sit for 30 minutes to allow the air bubbles to dissipate. Using a spoon, skim any remaining air bubbles from the surface.

To make the marbles, scoop ¼ tsp (1 ml) of the patchouli and amaro mixture into the sodium alginate bath. Repeat with the remaining mixture. Let sit in the bath for 5 minutes, or until the mixture has risen and created small spheres.

Use a slotted spoon to carefully transfer the marbles to the water rinse bath; to prevent the marbles from sticking together in the patchouli bath, make sure to thoroughly rid the marbles of alginate by agitating them in the water bath, then rinsing off before transferring to the patchouli bath.

Transfer the marbles to the patchouli bath and let steep for 1 hour or so. Store the marbles in the patchouli bath in the fridge for up to 2 days.

Inspired Sips

Toasted flavors here follow the glow from Night Blossom's bourbon and almond notes.

Bright Days

Makes 1 • Glass: Double old-fashioned

1 ½ oz (45 ml) reposado tequila
1 oz (30 ml) almond orgeat
¼ oz (8 ml) amaretto
¼ oz (8 ml) Amaro Montenegro
¼ oz (8 ml) Star Anise Syrup (p. 21)
⅛ oz (4 ml) pastis
King ice cube
Orange peel, to garnish

Pour the tequila, orgeat, amaretto, Amaro Montenegro, syrup, and pastis into a shaker with ice. Shake for 2 seconds to chill. Using a fine cocktail strainer, strain over a king cube in a double old-fashioned glass. Gently squeeze the peel between your index finger and thumb to extract the oils into the cocktail. Rest the peel on the king ice cube. Serve.

Bourbon Complexities

Makes 1 • Glass: White wine

1 ½ oz (45 ml) bourbon
½ oz (15 ml) Rosemary Syrup (p. 21)
¼ oz (8 ml) Green Cardamom Maraschino (p. 19)
¼ oz (8 ml) Campari
¼ oz (8 ml) green Chartreuse
½ oz (15 ml) Lillet Blanc
Grapefruit peel, to garnish

Pour the bourbon, syrup, maraschino, Campari, Chartreuse, and Lillet Blanc into a mixing glass. Fill the mixing glass with ice and stir three times to chill. Using a chinois, fine-strain into a white wine glass. Gently squeeze the peel between your index finger and thumb to extract the oils into the cocktail. Discard the peel. Serve.

Jalisco Spring

Makes 1 • Glass: Wine

1 oz (30 ml) reposado tequila
¼ oz (8 ml) Saffron Brandy (p. 18)
¼ oz (8 ml) Madeira
¼ oz (8 ml) Amaro Montenegro
¼ oz (8 ml) Rosemary Syrup (p. 21)
¼ oz (8 ml) Toasted Chamomile and Saffron Bitters (p. 17)
Rosemary sprig, to garnish

Pour the tequila, brandy, Madeira, Amaro Montenegro, syrup, and bitters into a shaker with ice. Stir five times to chill. Using a fine cocktail strainer, strain into a wine glass. Garnish with a sprig of rosemary. Serve.

Pictured opposite: Jalisco Spring

Violets and Cacao

As winter gives way to spring, nature awakens. Snow melts and, through it, we observe the seemingly effortless beauty of sprouts breaking through the frozen earth, enveloped by its deep, musky scent as they reach toward the warmth of the sun. This cocktail embodies the essence of spring as it begins to stir: spruce tips hand-foraged at the start of the season lend a quenching refreshment, while the pairing of rosemary and violet along with the deep, dark tone of caraway and cacao intrigue the senses. Violets and Cacao is a truly visceral composition, transforming in front of the guest's own eyes as the flavored snow melts into the pile of earth.

Makes 1
Glass: Stemless wine

PLATING

- 10 × 10 × 3-inch (25 × 25 × 8 cm) glass box
- 2 lb (907 g) black earth
- 3-inch (8 cm) diameter glass bowl
- 1 glass votive
- Demitasse spoon
- 1 small pot violets in soil

- 2 tbsp (30 ml) ground cacao nibs
- 5 tbsp Neutral Snow (p. 62)
- 12 long-stemmed basil sprouts
- 6–8 basil sprigs
- 3 tbsp (45 ml) Violet Cream Pearls (p. 62)
- 1 tbsp (15 ml) Blackberry Cells (p. 62)
- 1 tsp (5 ml) Cacao Cream and Caraway Fluid Gel (p. 62)
- 1 tsp (5 ml) Violet Fluid Gel (p. 63)
- Micro basil, to garnish
- 3 tbsp (45 ml) Cacao and Caraway Carbonic Snow (p. 63)

COCKTAIL

- Glass serving carafe

- 1½ oz (45 ml) Spruce Tip Gin (p. 18)
- ¼ oz (8 ml) violet liqueur
- ¼ oz (8 ml) Rosemary Syrup (p. 21)
- ¼ oz (8 ml) Rosemary and Lavender Bitters (p. 17)

To plate: Fill the glass box with the black earth. Use a wine glass to create a divot in the soil for the cocktail to rest in. Place half of the cacao nibs in the divot to act as a coaster. Create a second coaster with the remaining cacao nibs at the back left for the carafe.

Place the glass bowl in the back right corner of the box. Place the glass votive at the front right of the box, to hold the demitasse spoon. Lastly, place the carafe in the back left corner.

Scoop the neutral snow into piles scattered around the black earth. Garnish the service piece with 10 long-stemmed basil sprouts placed throughout the box, and place the potted violets in the back right corner.

Arrange the basil sprigs so that they "bloom" from the soil and snow.

In the glass bowl, scatter the pearls and cells. Place 5 dots of the cacao cream and caraway gel, and 4 dots of the violet gel on top of the pearls. Garnish the gels with micro basil.

Place 3 tbsp (45 ml) cacao and caraway snow in the wine glass and set at the front left of the service piece. Garnish the snow with the remaining 2 basil sprouts.

To compose the cocktail: Pour all the cocktail ingredients into a mixing glass with ice. Stir to chill, approximately three rotations.

To serve: Strain into a glass carafe and place the carafe on the "coaster" of cacao nibs.

Neutral Snow

Makes approximately 2 cups (500 ml)

2 cups (370 g) dry ice pellets (see p. 6)
1½ cups (375 ml) water

In a food processor, crush the dry ice pellets into a very fine dust, until the pieces are no larger than pea-sized, approximately 30 seconds. With the food processor on medium speed, slowly pour in the water. Turn off the food processor as soon as you have finished pouring. Store the snow in an airtight container in the freezer. It will last indefinitely.

Blackberry Cells

Makes ½ cup (125 ml)

Styrofoam container
Steel strainer

4 cups (1 L) liquid nitrogen
2 cups (500 ml) blackberries

Fill a Styrofoam container with liquid nitrogen. Carefully place the blackberries in a steel strainer submerged in the liquid nitrogen and leave for 30 seconds. (A steel strainer is critical here, since it is being submerged in the liquid nitrogen.) Using a spoon, carefully transfer the blackberries to a stainless-steel bowl. Put another stainless-steel bowl on top, upside down, to create a seal. Shake vigorously to separate the individual cells of the blackberries, then discard the white cores. Store in an airtight container in the freezer for up to 5 days.

Violet Cream Pearls

Makes approximately 1½ cups (375 ml)

Styrofoam container
Steel strainer

6¾ oz (200 ml) 10% cream
5 oz (150 ml) violet liqueur
4 g agar
8 cups (2 L) liquid nitrogen

In a medium pot over medium heat, bring the cream, violet liqueur, and agar to 200°F (93°C) and let simmer for just 5 seconds, to activate the agar. Carefully transfer the warm mixture to a squeeze bottle. Fill a Styrofoam container with liquid nitrogen. Place a large strainer inside the liquid nitrogen for 5 seconds to cool, then carefully squeeze drops of the violet cream into the liquid nitrogen to poach into pearls, using up all the mixture. Let the pearls rest in nitrogen for 10 to 15 seconds to freeze, shaking the strainer frequently to avoid the pearls from sticking to each other. Store in an airtight container in the freezer for up to 3 days.

Cacao Cream and Caraway Fluid Gel

Makes approximately 1½ cups (375 ml)

6¾ oz (200 ml) 10% cream
⅓ cup (98 ml) water
⅓ cup (98 ml) Caraway Maraschino (p. 19)
1 oz (28 g) Baker's bitter chocolate
3.5 g agar

In a medium pot over medium heat, bring all the ingredients to 200°F (93°C) for just 3 seconds to activate the agar. Pour into a plastic container and let set on a flat surface at room temperature, approximately 30 minutes. Using an immersion blender, blend the mixture until smooth. Store in a squeeze bottle in the fridge for up to 3 days.

Violet Fluid Gel

Makes approximately 2½ cups (375 ml)

- 6¾ oz (200 ml) violet liqueur
- 6¾ oz (200 ml) water
- 4.5 g agar

In a medium pot over medium heat, bring the liqueur, water, and agar to 201°F (94°C) for 3 seconds. Pour into a plastic container and let set on a flat surface at room temperature, approximately 45 minutes. Using an immersion blender, blend the mixture until smooth. Store in a squeeze bottle in the fridge for up to 3 days.

Cacao and Caraway Carbonic Snow

Makes approximately 2 cups (500 ml)

- 1 cup (250 ml) water
- ¾ oz (25 g) Baker's unsweetened chocolate
- 1 oz (30 ml) Caraway Maraschino (p. 19)
- ½ oz (15 ml) Star Anise Syrup (p. 21)
- 1 cup (185 g) dry ice pellets (see p. 6)

In a medium pot over low heat, heat the water and chocolate until the chocolate is completely melted, stirring and being careful not to burn it. Pour the mixture into a steel container and chill in the fridge overnight. Then use a chinois to strain 1 cup (250 ml) of the cacao water into a measuring container, and strain the remainder into an airtight container to store in the fridge for up to 3 days. Discard the sediment. (You can also freeze the leftover cacao water in ice cube molds, to use in your favorite Old-Fashioned recipe.)

To the measuring container with the cacao water, add the maraschino and syrup.

In a food processor, crush the dry ice pellets into a very fine dust, until the pieces are no larger than pea-sized, approximately 30 seconds. With the food processor on medium speed, slowly pour in the cacao-maraschino mixture. Turn off the food processor as soon as you have finished pouring. Store the snow in an airtight container for up to 3 days.

Inspired Sips

These florals, wood tones, and caramelized notes continue Violets and Cacao's journey into spring.

Kensington

Makes 1 • Glass: Wine

- 1¾ oz (50 ml) Canadian rye
- ¼ oz (8 ml) Patchouli Syrup (p. 21)
- ¼ oz (8 ml) Rosemary and Lavender Bitters (p. 17)
- ¼ oz (8 ml) violet liqueur
- ¼ oz (8 ml) sweet vermouth

Pour all the ingredients into a mixing glass with ice. Stir five times, or until chilled. Strain into a wine glass. Serve.

Spruce and Cacao

Makes 1 • Glass: Coupe

- 1½ oz (45 ml) Spruce Tip Gin (p. 18)
- ½ oz (15 ml) Madeira
- ½ oz (15 ml) Amaro Montenegro
- ¼ oz (8 ml) Star Anise Syrup (p. 21)
- ¼ oz (8 ml) Cocoa Bitters (p. 16)
- Grapefruit peel, to garnish
- Cedar sprig, to garnish

Pour the gin, Madeira, Amaro Montenegro, syrup, and cocoa bitters into a mixing glass with ice. Stir to chill. Using a chinois, fine-strain into a chilled coupe glass. Gently squeeze the peel between your index finger and thumb to extract the oils into the cocktail. Discard the peel. Garnish with the cedar sprig. Serve.

Montego Sour

Makes 1 • Glass: Coupe

- 1 g dried chamomile flowers
- 2 oz (60 ml) pineapple juice
- 1 oz (30 ml) amaretto
- ¾ oz (23 ml) fresh lemon juice
- ½ oz (15 ml) pastis
- ¼ oz (8 ml) Rosemary Syrup (p. 21)
- ¼ oz (8 ml) Toasted Chamomile and Saffron Bitters (p. 17)
- 1 egg white

In a frying pan over low heat, lightly toast the chamomile flowers until fragrant, approximately 15 minutes. Set aside.

Put the pineapple juice, amaretto, lemon juice, pastis, syrup, bitters, and egg white into a shaker. Shake for 5 seconds to aerate the egg white. Fill the shaker with ice and shake for another 5 seconds to chill. Using a cocktail strainer, fine-strain into a coupe glass. Place a piece of the toasted chamomile overtop. Serve.

Pictured opposite: Spruce and Cacao

SUMMER

Summer cocktails are all about bright, beautiful citrus and tropical fruit-forward compositions (think coconut and pineapple)—but also rhubarb, strawberry, and the crisp and refreshing flavors of cucumber and fresh mint. After all, the best part of the season is its abundance of seasonal fruits and vegetables and fresh herbs. All of this seasonality—including florals like lavender—is celebrated throughout this chapter, along with the refreshing qualities of compositions using various ices, such as flavored pearls, sherbets, and ice components. The cocktails in this chapter are meant to challenge both the industry mixologist and at-home drinker with interesting textures and the manipulation of ingredients while maintaining the essence of approachability with flavor combinations—basil and cucumber, coconut and lime, as well as some unexpectedly delicious pairings like tomato and strawberry.

Absinthe and Orange Blossom Frappé

Makes 1
Glass: Thin collins

PLATING

Ceramic bowl

- 1 Lemon Cream Bâtonnet (p. 72)
- 5 edible marigold petals
- Approximately 8 micro basil sprouts
- 2 tsp (10 ml) Orange Cells (p. 72)
- 1 tbsp (15 ml) Lemon and Chamomile Fluid Gel (p. 73)
- 1 tsp (5 ml) Elderflower Ice Pearls (p. 73)
- 1 tbsp (15 ml) Orange Blossom Crème Fraîche (p. 72)
- 1 tbsp (15 ml) Green Cardamom and Chartreuse Cream Fluid Gel (p. 73)
- 1 tsp (5 ml) Lemon and Thyme Cells (p. 73)
- 1 Coconut and Absinthe Bonbon (p. 74)
- 2 tbsp (30 ml) orange blossom water
- 1 cup (250 ml) boiled water
- 3 tbsp (30 g) dry ice pellets (see p. 6)

COCKTAIL

Glass serving carafe

- Approximately 2 cups (500 ml) Orange Blossom Crushed Ice (p. 73)
- 1½ oz (45 ml) coconut rum
- ½ oz (15 ml) Thyme Syrup (p. 21)
- ¼ oz (8 ml) Pernod French absinthe
- ¼ oz (8 ml) Green Cardamom Maraschino (p. 19)
- ⅙ oz (5 ml) Pernod pastis
- 10 marigold petals
- 1 oz (30 ml) soda water
- Confectioners' sugar, for dusting
- Micro basil, to garnish

A cocktail concept that truly embodies the idea of the creative process, and the power of inspiration from your surroundings. As I have learned over the years, the key to being a creative individual is allowing yourself to be present and open to perception and inspiration, and being mindful about grasping onto new ideas when they appear, especially in the context of a specific application. Perhaps you find that an aroma while eating a particular food item at a café inspires certain flavor and aromatic pairings, and that walking through a forest on a summer's day inspires certain tactile and immersive qualities of a service-piece design. This cocktail captures this approach to inspiration in a beautiful and elegant way.

During a recent family trip to Florida, I took my eldest son and my wife to an orange grove near where we were staying, hoping to pick fresh oranges. To our surprise, the trees were all in bloom. Entering the grove, I was overwhelmed by the captivating scent of fresh orange blossoms, the vibrancy of the distinct yellow-green leaves, and the beautiful white flowers (which all inspired this cocktail's color composition). At the end of the walk, we were greeted by merchant booths selling souvenirs as well as the orchard's signature orange and vanilla ice cream beverage. The drink was absolutely delicious, and enjoying it paired with the scent of the orchard's orange blossoms, I knew that I needed to create a modernist concept reflecting this experience. Absinthe, in my mind, naturally pairs with the flavors and aroma of orange and cream. Think classic Creamsicle meets absinthe frappé.

To plate: Position the bâtonnet lengthwise in the center of the ceramic bowl. Using a pin, poke six evenly spaced ½-inch (1 cm) deep holes in the bâtonnet. Alternate filling the holes with a marigold petal and a micro basil sprout.

On either side of the bâtonnet, place 1 tsp (5 ml) of the orange cells in a pile, then 1 dot approximately ¾ inch (2 cm) in diameter of the lemon and chamomile gel. Garnish each gel dot with a marigold petal.

Place the pearls at the base of the bâtonnet. Squeeze dots of orange blossom crème fraîche throughout the plate, then do the same with the green cardamom and Chartreuse cream gel. Garnish each dot of the cardamom gel with a micro basil sprout.

Distribute the remaining 1 tsp (5 ml) of orange cells in a pile on each side of the bâtonnet. Place the lemon and thyme cells below the orange cells to the left of the bâtonnet. Lastly, place the bonbon on top of the pile of orange cells to the right of the bâtonnet. Squeeze 1 dot of green cardamom fluid gel on top, then adhere a micro basil sprout to it, as garnish.

continued

To compose the cocktail: Fill a collins glass three-quarters of the way with the orange blossom ice. Pour the rum, syrup, absinthe, maraschino, and pastis into a shaker with ice. Shake for 5 seconds to chill. Using a Hawthorne strainer, strain over the orange blossom ice. Add the marigold petals and stir throughout the cocktail. Add the soda water and top with the orange blossom ice so that a mound of it pokes out of the glass. Dust the cocktail with confectioners' sugar and garnish with micro basil.

To serve: Put the orange blossom water with the boiled water in a carafe. Carefully add the dry ice pellets to activate the aromatic mist.

Present the activated aromatics and the cocktail at the 2 o'clock position in front of your guest. Carefully tip the aromatic carafe to allow the mist to fill the plate, essentially garnishing it with aroma.

Orange Blossom Crème Fraîche

Makes approximately 2 cups (500 ml)

- 2 cups (500 ml) buttermilk
- 2 cups (500 ml) 35% cream
- ½ oz (15 ml) fresh lemon juice
- 1¼ oz (38 ml) orange blossom water

In a measuring container, mix the buttermilk, cream, and lemon juice, stirring thoroughly for 5 minutes, until the mixture curdles. Cover and let sit at room temperature for 3 days, until it solidifies and there is a separation.

Using a chinois lined with cheesecloth, pour the mixture into the cheesecloth. Cover with plastic wrap and let sit in the fridge overnight. Remove the solids (crème fraîche) from the filter and discard the liquid.

Scoop 1 cup (250 ml) of the crème fraîche into a squeeze bottle. (You can store the remainder in the fridge for up to 10 days and use in place of sour cream.) Add the orange blossom water to the squeeze bottle and stir. Store in the fridge for up to 1 week.

Lemon Cream Bâtonnet

Makes approximately 12

- 6¾ oz (200 ml) Limoncello
- 5 oz (150 ml) 10% cream
- 2 oz (60 ml) orange blossom water
- ½ oz (15 ml) Pernod pastis
- 3 g agar

In a small pot over medium heat, bring all the ingredients to 190°F (88°C) and let simmer for 3 seconds, to activate the agar. Pour into a quarter pan and let set on a flat surface at room temperature, approximately 45 minutes. Carefully remove from the pan and cut into bâtonnets measuring 3 × ¾ inches (8 × 2 cm) each. Store in a parchment paper–lined airtight container in the fridge for up to 3 days.

Orange Cells

Makes approximately 3 tbsp (45 ml)

Styrofoam container

- 1 orange
- 4 cups (1 L) liquid nitrogen

Peel the orange and carefully segment, removing the pith. Fill a Styrofoam container with liquid nitrogen. Place the segments into the liquid nitrogen and poach for 30 seconds. Transfer the segments to a stainless-steel bowl and, using a pestle, apply pressure to separate any cells that have frozen together. Store in an airtight container in the freezer for up to 3 days.

Lemon and Chamomile Fluid Gel

Makes approximately 2 cups (500 ml)

- 2 cups (500 ml) water
- 1 cup (205 g) white sugar
- ¼ cup (8 g) dried chamomile flowers
- Peel from 2 lemons
- 3–5 g agar

In a medium pot over medium heat, bring the water, sugar, chamomile, and lemon peels to 194°F (90°C). Let simmer for 15 minutes. Remove from the heat and, using an immersion blender, carefully blend the mixture until smooth and the peel is pulverized. Using a chinois, fine-strain into a measuring container.

Return the mixture to the pot, adding 1 g agar per 3½ oz (105 ml) of the mixture. Bring to 200°F (93°C) and let simmer for just 5 seconds, to activate the agar. Pour into a steel container and let set on a flat surface at room temperature until firm to the touch, approximately 1 hour. Using an immersion blender, blend the mixture until smooth. Store in a squeeze bottle in the fridge for up to 3 days.

Elderflower Ice Pearls

Makes approximately 2 cups (500 ml)

2 Styrofoam containers

- 1⅓ cups (350 ml) elderflower soda (I prefer Bottle Green)
- 5 oz (150 ml) St-Germain
- ¼ oz (7 g) agar
- 8 cups (2 L) liquid nitrogen

In a small pot, bring the soda, St-Germain, and agar to 200°F (93°C) for 5 seconds, to activate the agar. While warm, pour into a squeeze bottle. Fill a Styrofoam container with liquid nitrogen and carefully squeeze drops of the elderflower mixture into the liquid nitrogen to poach into pearls, using up all the mixture. Using a fine strainer to capture the pearls, pour the contents from the Styrofoam container into another Styrofoam container. Store the pearls in an airtight container in the freezer for up to 3 days.

Green Cardamom and Chartreuse Cream Fluid Gel

Makes approximately 1 cup (250 ml)

- 5 oz (150 ml) 10% cream
- 1¾ oz (50 ml) Green Cardamom Maraschino (p. 19)
- 1¾ oz (50 ml) green Chartreuse
- 1¼ oz (35 g) Baker's white chocolate
- 3 g agar

In a medium pot over medium heat, bring all the ingredients to 190°F (88°C) and let simmer for 3 seconds, to activate the agar. Pour into a steel container and let set on a flat surface at room temperature, approximately 45 minutes. Using an immersion blender, blend the mixture until smooth. Store in a squeeze bottle in the fridge for up to 3 days.

Lemon and Thyme Cells

Makes approximately 2 tbsp (30 ml)

Styrofoam container

- 1 lemon
- ½ cup (125 ml) Thyme Syrup (p. 21)
- 4 cups (1 L) liquid nitrogen

Peel the lemon and carefully segment, removing the pith. Place in an airtight container with the syrup, then leave overnight in the fridge to macerate. Fill a Styrofoam container with liquid nitrogen. Poach the segments in the liquid nitrogen for 30 seconds. Transfer to a stainless-steel bowl and, using a pestle, apply pressure to carefully separate any cells that have frozen together. Store in an airtight container in the freezer for up to 3 days.

Orange Blossom Crushed Ice

Makes approximately 2 cups (500 ml)

- 2 cups (500 ml) ice
- 1 tbsp (15 ml) orange blossom water

In a food processor on medium speed, crush the ice into chunks (avoid over-processing into a dust). Transfer to an airtight container and stir in the orange blossom water until incorporated. Store in the freezer for up to 2 days.

Coconut and Absinthe Bonbons

Makes approximately 10

Twenty 1-inch (2.5 cm) demisphere molds

2½ oz (75 ml) 10% cream

1¾ oz (50 ml) coconut rum

½ oz (15 ml) coconut milk

½ oz (15 ml) orange blossom water

¼ oz (8 ml) Pernod absinthe

0.1 g xanthan gum

7 oz (200 g) cacao butter

5 oz (140 g) Baker's white chocolate

To make the filling, using an immersion blender, blend the cream, rum, coconut milk, orange blossom water, absinthe, and xanthan gum in a measuring container until evenly distributed and smooth. Pour into a third pan and let sit to release any air bubbles, approximately 30 minutes.

Pour the filling into the demisphere molds and freeze on a flat surface for 2 hours, until frozen solid.

Remove the frozen fillings from their molds. Hold one piece in each hand and, using a ceramic plate, rub the flat side of the demisphere on it to smooth into a flat, even edge. Hold the flat sides of two demispheres together and run your fingertip along the seam to seal them and smooth out any imperfections. Store in an airtight container in the freezer to maintain their shape.

To make the bonbon casings, prepare a double boiler: Place a stainless-steel bowl atop a small pot filled halfway with water over medium heat (the bowl should be the same circumference as the pan). Melt the cacao butter and white chocolate in the bowl, stirring frequently to evenly incorporate. Keep warm.

Poke a pin into a frozen sphere and submerge twice in the melted cacao butter to thoroughly coat. Remove the pin and place the sphere in a demisphere mold to maintain its shape. Repeat with the remaining spheres. Gently scrape a paring knife where the pin was to remove excess chocolate. Using a pin, dip the tip into the melted cocoa butter mixture and fill the hole. Store in an airtight container in the fridge for up to 3 days. Let sit at room temperature to thaw for 30 minutes before serving.

Inspired Sips

Absinthe and Orange Blossom Frappé's components display versatility in these deeply citrus and floral drinks.

Strawberry and Orange Blossom Julep

Makes 1 • Glass: Old-fashioned

- 1 cup (250 ml) Orange Blossom Crushed Ice (p. 73)
- 1½ oz (45 ml) Strawberry Gin (p. 18)
- ½ oz (15 ml) Saffron Brandy (p. 18)
- ½ oz (15 ml) Star Anise Syrup (p. 21)
- ¼ oz (8 ml) Madeira
- ¼ oz (8 ml) Toasted Chamomile and Saffron Bitters (p. 17)
- 2 stems mint

Place the orange blossom ice in an old-fashioned glass. Pour the gin, brandy, syrup, Madeira, and bitters into a mixing glass. Fill with ice and stir to chill, approximately three rotations. Strain over the orange blossom ice. Garnish with the mint. Serve.

Sage Garden

Makes 1 • Glass: White wine

- 1½ oz (45 ml) London dry gin
- ¼ oz (8 ml) Thyme Syrup (p. 21)
- ¼ oz (8 ml) late harvest Vidal
- ¼ oz (8 ml) Fennel and Chamomile Bitters (p. 16)
- ¼ oz (8 ml) Lavender Maraschino (p. 19)
- 4 sage leaves

Put all the ingredients into a mixing glass and muddle the sage thoroughly. Fill the glass with ice and stir to chill, approximately five rotations. Using a Hawthorne strainer, strain into a white wine glass. Serve.

Kentucky Evergreen

Makes 1 • Glass: White wine

- 1½ oz (45 ml) bourbon
- ½ oz (15 ml) Green Cardamom Maraschino (p. 19)
- ½ oz (15 ml) Madeira
- ¼ oz (8 ml) Thyme Syrup (p. 21)
- ¼ oz (8 ml) Balsam Fir Bitters (p. 16)
- Red grapefruit peel

Put all the ingredients except the peel into a mixing glass. Fill the mixing glass with ice and stir to chill, approximately three rotations. Using a Hawthorne strainer, fine-strain into a white wine glass. Gently squeeze the peel between your index finger and thumb to extract the oils into the cocktail. Discard the peel. Serve.

Pictured opposite: Sage Garden

Chilled Ontario Strawberry

This is one of my favorite expressions of the modernist approach to mixology that we at BarChef have utilized over the years, where cocktails are presented in a way that frames them as a culinary dish, rather than as a simple beverage. Using a footed bowl service piece here allows for the cocktail to be sipped or consumed with a spoon, raising the question of whether it is indeed a cocktail or a dish. Does alcohol content alone inform this? A large emphasis was placed on the texture of the base of this cocktail—a very loose gel. I wanted to create a soup-like texture to thicken the viscosity of the liquid and put emphasis on mouthfeel and complexity, allowing the vibrant aromatics of the cocktail to be picked up by the olfactory system. The inspiration behind the flavors? A chilled Ontario strawberry gazpacho. Celebrating my province's local strawberry, basil, and lavender, this is the embodiment of nostalgic summer flavors for me. I have childhood memories of strawberry picking with my mother during the summer, and can still taste the fresh strawberries that I bit into directly off the vine.

Nostalgia—in flavors, textures, and aromas—is an incredibly powerful resource for chefs and mixologists. Establishing these points of reference allows us to create visceral and emotional experiences for our guests, prompting their personal interpretation of these elements as they evoke nostalgic memories for them.

Makes 1
Glass: Footed ceramic or glass bowl

PLATING

Glass serving carafe

- 1 Violet Demisphere (p. 82)
- 1 Balsamic and Lavender Ribbon (p. 82)
- 1 tsp (5 ml) Lemon and Chamomile Brunoise (p. 83)
- 3 basil sprouts
- ½ oz (15 ml) Lavender Maraschino and Coconut Fluid Gel (p. 83)
- 4 g Roasted Black Pepper Sugar (p. 82)
- 1 cup (250 ml) Strawberry Gazpacho (p. 82)

To plate: In the footed bowl, place the demisphere at the 3 o'clock position.

Carefully wind the balsamic and lavender ribbon into a coil and place it toward the center of the bowl, near the demisphere.

Place the brunoise at the 12 o'clock position, and garnish with the basil sprouts.

Squeeze 5 dots of the lavender and coconut gel to trace the lefthand curve of the ribbon coil. Sprinkle the pepper sugar at the base of the ribbon.

Pour the strawberry gazpacho into a carafe. Place the carafe and a soup spoon on a small white plate in front of your guest.

To serve: Pour the gazpacho over the elements in the footed bowl.

Roasted Black Pepper Sugar

Makes approximately 1 cup (205 g)

- 2 g black peppercorns
- ½ cup (102 g) white sugar

Preheat the oven to 300°F (150°C). Scatter the peppercorns on a baking sheet and bake for 45 minutes, agitating frequently to make sure they do not burn. The peppercorns are ready when you can crush them between your fingers.

Using a mortar and pestle, grind the roasted peppercorns into a dust. In a stainless-steel bowl, place the sugar and 1 tsp (5 ml) pepper dust and stir (if you have extra pepper dust, keep it for seasoning when cooking). Store in an airtight container for up to 3 weeks.

Strawberry Gazpacho

Makes approximately 4 cups (1 L)

- 4 cups (1 L) water
- 1 lb (454 g) chopped fresh strawberries
- ½ cup (102 g) white sugar
- 10 oz (300 ml) Strawberry Gin (p. 18)
- 2.5 g agar

In a blender, blend the water, strawberries, and sugar until smooth. Using a metal-mesh strainer, strain into a measuring container, discarding the solids.

In a small pot over medium heat, bring 3½ oz (105 ml) of the strained liquid and the agar to 200°F (93°C) and let simmer for just 5 seconds, to activate the agar. Transfer the mixture along with the remainder of the blended mixture to a large stainless-steel bowl and stir to incorporate everything. Transfer to the fridge and let set for 1 hour, until the texture is soft but stable.

Add the gin to the mixture. Using an immersion blender, blend the mixture to a smooth soup-like consistency. Store in an airtight container in the fridge for up to 5 days. Serve chilled.

Violet Demisphere

Makes approximately 20

- *Twenty 1-inch (2.5 cm) demisphere molds*
- 5 oz (150 ml) violet liqueur
- 1¾ oz (50 ml) water
- 1 g agar

In a small pot over medium heat, bring the violet liqueur, water, and agar to 195°F (91°C) and let simmer for 3 seconds, to activate the agar. Pour into the demisphere molds and let set on a flat surface at room temperature. Store in a parchment paper–lined airtight container in the fridge for up to 3 days.

Balsamic and Lavender Ribbon

Makes approximately 10 ribbons

- 1 tbsp (15 ml) canola or seed oil
- 4 gelatin sheets
- 3½ oz (105 ml) Balsamic and Lavender Syrup (p. 20)

Lightly coat a quarter pan with the canola oil, then line the pan with plastic wrap.

Submerge the gelatin sheets in a bowl of ice-cold water for 30 seconds to bloom them. Then use your hands to squeeze the gelatin sheets to extract as much water as possible.

In a small pot over low heat, heat the bloomed gelatin sheets and the syrup until the gelatin dissolves. Pour into the prepared quarter pan and let set on a flat surface in the fridge for 1 hour.

Square up any rounded corners, then slice the gel into ten ½-inch (1 cm) wide ribbons. Store in a parchment paper–lined airtight container in the fridge for up to 3 days.

Lemon and Chamomile Brunoise

Makes approximately 2 cups (500 ml)

- 2 cups (500 ml) water
- 1 cup (205 g) white sugar
- ¼ cup (8 g) dried chamomile flowers
- Peels of 2 lemons
- 2 g agar

In a medium pot over medium heat, bring the water, sugar, chamomile, and peels to a simmer, and let simmer for 5 minutes. Remove from the heat and let cool.

Using an immersion blender, blend the mixture until smooth. Using a fine-mesh strainer, fine-strain into an airtight container.

In a small pot, bring 6¾ oz (200 ml) of the chamomile mixture and the agar to 200°F (93°C) and let simmer for just 5 seconds, to activate the agar. Pour into a 6 × 4-inch (15 × 10 cm) container and let set on a flat surface at room temperature for 1 hour, until firm to the touch.

Invert the container and, using your hands, carefully remove the set gel. Square up any rounded corners, then cut into ¼-inch (6 mm) cubes. Store in a parchment paper–lined airtight container in the fridge for up to 3 days.

Lavender Maraschino and Coconut Fluid Gel

Makes approximately 1 cup (250 ml)

- 6¾ oz (200 ml) coconut milk
- 1 oz (30 ml) Lavender Maraschino (p. 19)
- 1 oz (30 ml) Vanilla Syrup (p. 21)
- 0.5 g soy lecithin
- 2 g agar

Put the coconut milk, maraschino, syrup, and lecithin into a measuring container and, using an immersion blender, blend until evenly incorporated.

In a small pot, bring 3½ oz (105 ml) of the mixture and the agar to 198°F (92°C) and let simmer for just 5 seconds, to activate the agar. Add the remaining liquid and blend, using the immersion blender, until smooth. Pour into a large stainless-steel bowl and let set on a flat surface in the fridge until firm to the touch, approximately 1 hour.

Remove the mixture from the fridge and, using the immersion blender, blend again until smooth. Store in a squeeze bottle in the fridge for up to 3 days.

Inspired Sips

Fruit, herbs, brightness—the Chilled Ontario Strawberry lives on in these three drinks.

Aperol Strawberry Spritz

Makes 1 • Glass: Burgundy wine

- 1 oz (30 ml) Strawberry Gin (p. 18)
- 1 oz (30 ml) Thyme Syrup (p. 21)
- ½ oz (15 ml) Aperol
- ¼ oz (8 ml) Amaro Montenegro
- 1 oz (30 ml) sparkling wine
- 1 oz (30 ml) soda water
- Mint sprig, to garnish
- Grapefruit peel, to garnish

Pour the gin, syrup, Aperol, and Amaro Montenegro into a large Burgundy wine glass. Fill the glass with ice. Top with the sparkling wine and soda water and stir to chill. Garnish with the sprig of mint. Gently squeeze the peel between your index finger and thumb to extract the oils into the cocktail. Discard the peel. Serve.

Coconut Mojito

Makes 1 • Glass: Double old-fashioned

- 2 oz (60 ml) coconut rum
- 1½ oz (45 ml) fresh lime juice
- 1 oz (30 ml) Vanilla Syrup (p. 21)
- 1 oz (30 ml) coconut milk
- 2 mint sprigs
- 2 lime wheels

Put the rum, lime juice, syrup, coconut milk, the picked leaves from 1 mint sprig, and the lime wheels into a shaker and muddle. Add 4 or 5 ice cubes and shake. Pour the contents into a double old-fashioned glass. Garnish with the remaining mint sprig.

Provençal

Makes 1 • Glass: White wine

- 1½ oz (45 ml) London dry gin
- ¼ oz (8 ml) Lavender Maraschino (p. 19)
- ¼ oz (8 ml) dry vermouth
- ¼ oz (8 ml) Rosemary Syrup (p. 21)
- ¼ oz (8 ml) Balsam Fir Bitters (p. 16)
- Rosemary sprig, to garnish
- Grapefruit peel, to garnish

Pour the gin, lavender maraschino, vermouth, syrup, and bitters into a mixing glass. Fill the glass with ice and stir to chill. Strain into a white wine glass. Garnish with a sprig of rosemary. Gently squeeze the peel between your index finger and thumb to extract the oils into the cocktail. Discard the peel. Serve.

Pictured opposite: Aperol Strawberry Spritz

Day into Evening

Makes 1
Glass: Tulip Burgundy

PLATING

- 14 × 5-inch (35 × 13 cm) shallow rectangular glass vase
- Fresh wheatgrass in soil
- Black earth
- 7 × 3-inch (18 × 8 cm) glass plate
- ½-inch (1 cm) ring mold
- Atomizer

- 1 Chamomile and Bitter Almond Base (p. 90)
- 1 oz (30 ml) Green Grass and Chartreuse Cream (p. 90)
- 2 pieces dill flowers
- 2 tsp (10 ml) Strawberry Cream Gel (p. 90)
- 1 bunch micro basil
- 2 tsp (10 ml) Maple and Madeira Fluid Gel (p. 126)
- 1 bunch mint
- 2 tsp (10 ml) Islay Scotch and Rosemary Gel (p. 91)
- 6 ground cacao nibs
- ½ cup (125 ml) Green Grass Air (p. 43)
- ½ cup (125 ml) Hickory Air (p. 91)

COCKTAIL

- 1½ oz (45 ml) reposado tequila
- ½ oz (15 ml) Chamomile Syrup (p. 20)
- ¼ oz (8 ml) Fennel and Chamomile Bitters (p. 16)
- ¼ oz (8 ml) Luxardo maraschino
- ⅛ oz (4 ml) green Chartreuse
- 1 Toasted Chamomile, Cacao, and Rosemary Ice Sphere (p. 91)
- Orange blossom water, to garnish

The goal with this cocktail, incredibly ambitious as it was, was to have a composition presented with both edible and drinkable transformative experiences. Visuals capture the beautiful essence of a summer's day with vibrant green grass that contrasts with dark brown earth. This is one of my favorite qualities of progressive and contemporary composition: the use of natural elements in an unexpectedly pristine way, with stark lines and defined angles.

I have fond memories of enjoying many a summer's day at my in-laws, riding a dirt bike with my son, picking strawberries from the garden, barbecues and campfires in the evening with the beautiful orange glow of the setting sun on the horizon. This cocktail captures all those elements in both flavor and aroma, seemingly effortlessly.

To plate: Place the vase with a long side toward you. Cut a 2½-inch (6 cm) wide strip of the wheatgrass and place at the back of the vase. Cut another 2½-inch (6 cm) wide strip of wheatgrass and place on the right side of the vase, creating an L-shape.

Fill the vase with the black earth, packing it in firmly so that the wheatgrass strips stand upright. Wipe the exterior of the vase clean. Place the glass plate on top of the earth at the front left corner of the vase.

Place the chamomile and bitter almond base on a flat surface. Using the ring mold, cut 18 randomly placed holes in the base; it should look like Swiss cheese. Discard the cut pieces.

Carefully transfer the base to the glass plate, with the chamomile part on the left. Starting with the hole on the far left, fill 4 holes with the green grass and Chartreuse cream, then garnish 2 of these with dill flowers. Fill the next 4 holes with the strawberry cream gel, then garnish 2 of these with micro basil. Fill the next 4 holes with the maple and Madeira gel, then garnish 2 of these with mint. Fill the remaining 6 holes with the Islay Scotch and rosemary gel, then garnish these with the cacao nibs.

Place a dollop of green grass air on the far left side of the base, and a dollop of hickory air on the right-hand side of the base.

To compose the cocktail: Pour the tequila, syrup, bitters, maraschino, and Chartreuse into a mixing glass. Fill the mixing glass with ice and stir to chill, approximately three rotations. Place the ice sphere in the tulip Burgundy glass. Using a Hawthorne strainer, strain the cocktail over the ice sphere. Fill an atomizer with orange blossom water, and garnish the cocktail with a spritz of orange blossom water. Place the tulip glass at the back right of the vase.

To serve: Enjoy the edible components, working your way from left to right while intermittently sipping the cocktail

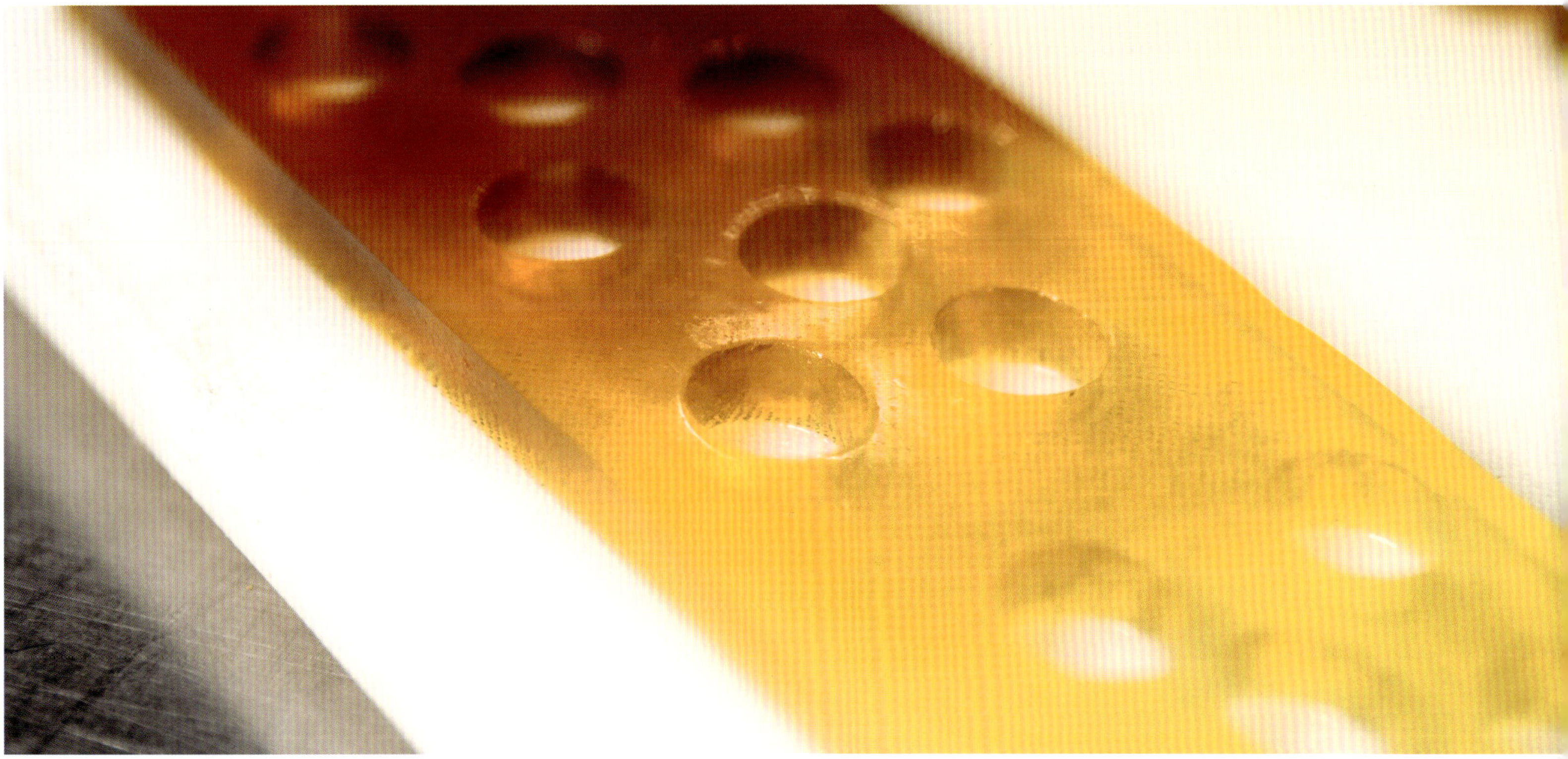

Green Grass and Chartreuse Cream

Makes approximately 1 cup (250 ml)

- 1 cup (250 ml) 10% cream
- ¾ oz (23 ml) green Chartreuse
- 1 cup (20 g) fresh wheatgrass
- 4 g white sugar
- 4 g agar

In a measuring container and using an immersion blender, blend all the ingredients except the agar until evenly distributed. Using a chinois, fine-strain into another measuring container.

In a small pot over medium heat, bring 3¼ oz (98 ml) of the mixture and the agar to 198°F (92°C) and let simmer for 3 seconds, to activate the agar. Add the remaining mixture and, using an immersion blender, blend until smooth. Pour into a steel container and let set on a flat surface at room temperature, approximately 1 hour. Using an immersion blender, blend the mixture until smooth. Store in a squeeze bottle in the fridge for up to 3 days.

Strawberry Cream Gel

Makes approximately 1½ cups (375 ml)

- 6¾ oz (200 ml) Strawberry Gin (p. 18)
- 6¾ oz (200 ml) 10% cream
- 1 tbsp (12 g) white sugar
- 5 g agar

In a medium pot over medium heat, stir together all the ingredients, bringing to 195°F (91°C). Pour into a steel container and let set on a flat surface at room temperature until firm to the touch, approximately 30 minutes. Using an immersion blender, blend the mixture until smooth. Store in a squeeze bottle in the fridge for up to 3 days.

Toasted Chamomile, Cacao, and Rosemary Ice Spheres

Makes 6

- *Six 2½-inch (6 cm) spherical ice molds*
- 3⅕ cups (800 ml) water
- 1¾ oz (50 g) Baker's dark chocolate
- 3¼ oz (98 ml) Rosemary Syrup (p. 21)
- 1¾ oz (50 ml) Toasted Chamomile and Saffron Bitters (p. 17)

In a medium pot over low heat, stir together the water and Baker's chocolate until the chocolate is melted and smooth. Pour into a container and chill overnight in the fridge.

The following day, using a chinois, strain the chocolate mixture into a measuring container, discarding the sediment. Add the syrup and bitters. Stir to mix thoroughly, then pour into the molds. Freeze thoroughly before using. Store in the freezer for up to 3 days.

Islay Scotch and Rosemary Gel

Makes 1 cup (250 ml)

- 6¾ oz (200 ml) Rosemary Syrup (p. 21)
- 3½ oz (105 ml) Islay Scotch
- 3½ oz (105 ml) water
- 5 g agar

In a medium pot over medium heat, bring all the ingredients to 192°F (89°C). Pour into a steel container and let set on a flat surface at room temperature until firm to the touch, approximately 1 hour. Using an immersion blender, blend the mixture until smooth. Store in a squeeze bottle in the fridge for up to 3 days.

Chamomile and Bitter Almond Bases

Makes 3

- ¾ cup + 3 tbsp (225 ml) water
- 5 oz (150 ml) Chamomile Syrup (p. 20)
- 5 g agar
- 6½ oz (140 ml) Disaronno amaretto
- 1¼ oz (38 ml) Averna amaro
- 0.25 g xanthan gum

In a measuring container, combine the ¾ cup (180 ml) of water, the syrup, and 3 g of the agar. Using an immersion blender, blend until mixed.

In a medium pot over medium heat, bring 1¼ cups (300 ml) of the chamomile mixture to 201°F (94°C), letting it simmer for 1 second. Remove from the heat and let the temperature reduce to 150°F (65°C), approximately 10 minutes.

Meanwhile, in a measuring container, combine the remaining 3 tbsp (45 ml) water with 2 g agar, amaretto, amaro, and xanthan gum. Using an immersion blender, blend until the xanthan gum is dissolved. Let sit for 30 seconds, or until the air is fully dispersed.

In a medium pot over medium heat, bring the amaretto mixture to 187°F (86°C) while stirring, then let simmer for 3 seconds, to activate the agar. Remove from the heat and let the temperature lower to 150°F (65°C), approximately 10 minutes.

With the chamomile mixture at 150°F (65°C) and the amaretto mixture at 150°F (65°C), very slowly and at the same time pour both mixtures into opposite ends of a half pan. The mixtures will meet to create a gradual two-tone base. If done correctly, the bitter almond base will cover one-third of the pan, and the chamomile base two-thirds. This does take some practice but the result is truly magnificent.

Let sit for 30 minutes at room temperature to set. Carefully transfer the gel to a clean work surface. Square up any rounded corners, then cut the gel into three 7½ × 2½-inch (19 × 6 cm) strips. Store in an airtight container in the fridge for up to 2 days.

Hickory Air

Makes 4 cups (1 L)

Blowtorch
6½ oz (185 g) hickory chips

- 4 cups (1 L) water
- 2 tsp (8 g) white sugar
- 1 g soy lecithin

Set up a smoking tray: Pour the water and sugar into a stainless-steel bowl and stir to dissolve the sugar. Keep close by.

Put the hickory chips into a steel baking tray, then use the blowtorch to ignite them so that they become glowing embers; extinguish any flames by covering the hickory chips with an upside-down pan. Nestle the bowl of sugar water in the burning embers and enclose with another steel pan to smoke the water for 30 seconds.

Using a chinois, fine-strain the smoked water into a deep quarter pan. Add the soy lecithin. Using an immersion blender, blend until the lecithin is evenly distributed. Blend the surface of the mixture to create a foam. Let sit for 15 seconds, then use immediately.

Inspired Sips

These cocktails are key to winding down, echoing the chamomile glow of Day into Evening.

Sparkling Paloma

Makes 1 • Glass: Collins

1 oz (30 ml) reposado tequila
1 oz (30 ml) Thyme Syrup (p. 21)
¼ oz (8 ml) Fennel and Chamomile Bitters (p. 16)
2 fresh grapefruit segments
3½ oz (105 ml) sparkling grapefruit soda
Lemon peel, to garnish

Pour the tequila, syrup, and bitters into a collins glass. Fill the glass with ice and stir to chill, approximately three rotations. Add the grapefruit segments and top with the grapefruit soda. Gently squeeze the peel between your index finger and thumb to extract the oils into the cocktail. Discard the peel. Serve.

Toasted Whisky Sour

Makes 1 • Glass: Coupe

1½ oz (45 ml) Canadian rye
1 oz (30 ml) Chamomile Syrup (p. 20)
¾ oz (23 ml) fresh lemon juice
¼ oz (8 ml) Toasted Chamomile and Saffron Bitters (p. 17)
⅛ oz (4 ml) pastis
1 egg white
Orange peel, to garnish

Put all the ingredients except the orange peel into a shaker and shake to aerate the egg white. Fill the shaker with ice and shake for 5 seconds to chill. Using a fine cocktail strainer, strain into a coupe glass. Gently squeeze the peel between your index finger and thumb to extract the oils into the cocktail. Discard the peel. Serve.

Mojave Spritz

Makes 1 • Glass: Collins

1¼ oz (38 ml) Saffron Brandy (p. 18)
1 oz (30 ml) fresh lemon juice
¾ oz (23 ml) Chamomile Syrup (p. 20)
½ oz (15 ml) amaretto
⅛ oz (4 ml) pastis
2 mint sprigs
2 oz (60 ml) soda water
Orange peel, to garnish

Pour the brandy, lemon juice, syrup, amaretto, and pastis into a collins glass. Add the leaves from 1 mint sprig and muddle. Fill the glass with ice and stir to chill, approximately three rotations. Top with soda, then garnish with the remaining mint sprig. Gently squeeze the peel between your index finger and thumb to extract the oils into the cocktail. Discard the peel. Serve.

Pictured opposite: Toasted Whisky Sour

Fields of Grain

Makes 1
Glass: Stemless goblet

This cocktail utilizes illumination to emphasize and accentuate the detailed texture in the canopy of dried grains that surrounds the edible components. It's a technique used in a few of my compositions to bring attention to various elements. Here, the glass beading with the towering grains creates a wonderful amber and orange glow resembling a beautiful sunset over Canadian grain fields.

PLATING

- Floral foam
- 14 × 5-inch (35 × 13 cm) bamboo bento box
- 2 battery-operated LED lights
- Amber glass beads
- 48 pieces 14-inch (35 cm) long dried grain
- Glass bowl
- Styrofoam container
- 2 oz (60 ml) ladle

- ¼ cup (60 ml) Saffron and Bitter Almond Snow (p. 96)
- 1 tbsp (15 ml) Orange Cells (p. 72)
- 8 cups (2 L) liquid nitrogen
- 1 cup (250 ml) Amaro Cream Espuma (p. 96)
- 2 tbsp (30 ml) Campari and Rosemary Fluid Gel (p. 97)
- 2 tbsp (30 ml) Islay Scotch and Star Anise Fluid Gel (p. 97)
- 1 marigold
- 1 sheet gold leaf

COCKTAIL

- Serving carafe

- 1½ oz (45 ml) Canadian rye
- 1 oz (30 ml) ginger beer
- ½ oz (15 ml) Amaro Montenegro
- ½ oz (15 ml) Rosemary Syrup (p. 21)
- ¼ oz (8 ml) Toasted Chamomile and Saffron Bitters (p. 17)
- 3 tbsp (45 ml) Orange Blossom Crushed Ice (p. 73)
- 1 Saffron Ice Cube (p. 96)
- 2 mint sprigs

To plate: To set up the service piece, fit the floral foam into the bento box to ½ inch (1 cm) below its lip. Place an LED light on the foam on either side of the bento box and press down so that the light is flush with the foam. Cover with the amber glass beads. Stand the stalks of grain along the back and sides of the bento box.

Put the snow into a glass bowl, then top with the orange cells.

Fill a Styrofoam container with the liquid nitrogen. Submerge the ladle in the liquid nitrogen until the "boiling" subsides. Then remove the ladle and fill with the amaro espuma, using an offset spatula to scrape across the top and remove any excess, creating a flat edge. Slowly submerge the ladle in the liquid nitrogen. Keep it submerged until the espuma releases from the ladle and floats in the nitrogen. Let poach for 10 seconds to freeze thoroughly. Transfer the frozen espuma to the glass, with the domed side facing upward, to resemble the setting sun.

Slowly squeeze 3 dots of the Campari gel onto the espuma and the snow surrounding it (squeezing slowly allows the gel to freeze to the espuma). Squeeze 3 dots of the Scotch and star anise gel onto the espuma and the snow surrounding it. Garnish the dots with marigold petals. Finally, squeeze 1 dot of the Campari gel in the center of the espuma, and garnish with gold leaf.

To compose the cocktail: Pour the rye, ginger beer, amaro, syrup, and bitters into a carafe and stir.

To serve: Put the orange blossom crushed ice into a stemless wine glass. Place the saffron ice cube on top. Garnish with the mint. Arrange the wine glass on the far left side of the service piece, over an LED light. Serve tableside by pouring the cocktail from the carafe into the wine glass.

Saffron Ice Cubes

Makes 3 king cubes

King cube mold

10½ oz (315 ml) water

1¾ oz (50 ml) Saffron Brandy (p. 18)

In a measuring container, stir together the water and brandy. Pour into the king cube molds. Freeze thoroughly before using. Store in the freezer for up to 5 days.

Saffron and Bitter Almond Snow

Makes approximately 2 cups (500 ml)

6¾ oz (200 ml) water

3½ oz (105 ml) Saffron Brandy (p. 18)

2½ oz (75 ml) Star Anise Syrup (p. 21)

1¾ oz (50 ml) amaretto

2 cups (370 g) dry ice pellets (see p. 6)

In a measuring container, combine the water, saffron brandy, syrup, and amaretto.

In a food processor, crush the dry ice pellets into a very fine dust, until the pieces are no larger than pea-sized, approximately 30 seconds. With the food processor on medium speed, slowly pour in the brandy mixture. Turn off the food processor as soon as you have finished pouring. Store the snow in an airtight container in the freezer for up to 3 days.

Amaro Cream Espuma

Makes approximately 2 cups (500 ml)

iSi siphon and charger (see p. 8)

7½ oz (225 ml) 10% cream

5 oz (150 ml) Amaro Montenegro

1¾ oz (50 ml) Star Anise Syrup (p. 21)

1 oz (30 ml) orange blossom water

1 sheet gelatin

Prepare an ice bath.

Heat all the ingredients in a small pot over medium heat, stirring to dissolve the gelatin. Transfer to the iSi siphon, close, and shake vigorously for 1 minute, then charge with the nitrous oxide charger. Place the siphon in the ice bath and let sit for 1 hour to set. Remove and store in the fridge for up to 3 days.

Campari and Rosemary Fluid Gel

Makes approximately 13 tbsp (195 ml)

- 7 tbsp (105 ml) Rosemary Syrup (p. 21)
- 1¾ oz (50 ml) water
- 1¾ oz (50 ml) Campari
- 3 g agar

In a medium pot over medium heat, bring all the ingredients to 200°F (93°C) and let simmer for just 15 seconds, to activate the agar. Pour into a steel container and let set on a flat surface at room temperature until firm to the touch, approximately 1 hour. Using an immersion blender, blend the mixture until smooth. Store in a squeeze bottle in the fridge for up to 3 days.

Islay Scotch and Star Anise Fluid Gel

Makes ¾ cup (180 ml)

- 1¾ oz (50 ml) Star Anise Syrup (p. 21)
- 2½ oz (75 ml) water
- 1 oz (30 ml) Islay Scotch
- 1 oz (30 ml) Toasted Chamomile and Saffron Bitters (p. 17)
- 2 g agar

In a medium pot over medium heat, bring all the ingredients to 200°F (93°C) for 15 seconds. Pour into a steel container to let set at room temperature until firm to the touch, approximately 1 hour. Using an immersion blender, blend the mixture until smooth. Store in a squeeze bottle in the fridge for up to 3 days.

Inspired Sips

Fields of Grain's warmth makes a home in these drinks with star anise and toasted chamomile.

Jalisco Sour

Makes 1 • Glass: Coupe

1½ oz (45 ml) reposado tequila
¾ oz (23 ml) fresh lemon juice
½ oz (15 ml) Campari
½ oz (15 ml) Star Anise Syrup (p. 21)
¼ oz (8 ml) amaretto
1 egg white
Orange peel, to garnish
Piece star anise, to garnish

Put all the ingredients except the orange peel and star anise into a shaker, and shake for approximately 5 seconds to aerate the egg white. Fill the shaker with ice and shake for 2 seconds to chill. Using a Hawthorne strainer, fine-strain into a coupe glass. Gently squeeze the peel between your index finger and thumb to extract the oils into the cocktail. Discard the peel. Add a piece of star anise in the center of the cocktail. Serve.

Apricot and Amaretto Sour

Makes 1 • Glass: Cocktail

1¼ oz (38 ml) Apricot Brandy (p. 18)
1 oz (30 ml) Star Anise Syrup (p. 21)
¾ oz (23 ml) fresh lemon juice
½ oz (15 ml) amaretto
¼ oz (8 ml) Toasted Chamomile and Saffron Bitters (p. 17)
1 egg white
Orange peel, to garnish

Put all the ingredients except the orange peel into a shaker. Dry shake to aerate the egg white. Add ice and shake for 2 seconds to chill. Using a Hawthorne strainer, fine-strain into a cocktail glass. Gently squeeze the peel between your index finger and thumb to extract the oils into the cocktail. Discard the peel. Serve.

Cedar and Saffron Old-Fashioned

Makes 1 • Glass: Old-fashioned

1¾ oz (50 ml) Cedar Rye (p. 19)
¼ oz (8 ml) Rosemary Syrup (p. 21)
¼ oz (8 ml) Toasted Chamomile and Saffron Bitters (p. 17)
3 peels orange
King ice cube

Put the rye, syrup, bitters, and 2 orange peels into an old-fashioned glass. Muddle the orange peels. Add the king cube and stir to chill, approximately three rotations. Garnish the cocktail with a flamed orange peel: Hold a lit match beside the cocktail in one hand and the remaining orange peel in the other. Squeeze the peel between your index finger and thumb toward the match, igniting oils from the peel. Discard the peel. Serve.

Pictured opposite: Jalisco Sour

Heirloom Caesar

This cocktail is a visual deconstruction of the iconic Canadian classic: the Caesar. Rather than having all the components mixed in one glass, however, they are prepared individually so that when the cocktail is poured, they integrate to create the final composition. The heirloom nature is thanks to the cocktail's multicolor composition: purples, reds, and oranges can all be found here. I chose ingredients that provide structure and complexity, ones that showcase the flavor profiles of the infused vodka base: thyme to pair with the celery snow, pickled beet to pair with the fried capers, and so on. The tomato water's umami finish leaves a deliciously intriguing flavor profile on the palate, with the snows incorporating aromatics when they're activated tableside. Through the various gelification techniques, we achieve thought-provoking textures for flavors that would typically appear in other forms, such as pickled beet, making this concoction a truly exceptional adaptation of the original.

Makes 1
Glass: Tall glass bowl, approximately 6 × 4 inches (15 × 10 cm) (the tomato ice bowl must be able to sit on its mouth)

COCKTAIL

Serving carafe

- 3 oz (90 ml) Spiced Vodka Infusion (p. 19)
- ½ cup (125 ml) Tomato Water (p. 102)
- 1 pinch smoked Maldon salt

PLATING

- 1 tbsp (15 ml) Clamato Snow (p. 102)
- 2 tbsp (30 ml) Celery Snow (p. 103)
- 1 pinch smoked Maldon salt
- 1 tbsp (15 ml) Pickled Beet Brunoise (p. 102)
- 8 basil sprouts
- 6 small curly parsley leaves
- Tomato Ice Bowl (p. 102)
- 1 tbsp (15 ml) green peas
- 4 Deep-Fried Capers (p. 103)
- 1 tbsp (15 ml) grated horseradish

To compose the cocktail: In a small pot over low heat, heat the vodka infusion, tomato water, and salt while you plate the remaining components.

To plate: While the tomato vodka water heats, place the Clamato snow and celery snow in a tall glass bowl. Add the salt. Place the brunoise, 4 basil sprouts, and 3 of the parsley leaves on top of the snow.

Sit the tomato ice bowl in the mouth of the glass bowl. Place the green peas in the center of the tomato ice bowl and garnish with the remaining 4 basil sprouts, 3 parsley leaves, and the capers. Place the horseradish in a pile at the base of the bowl.

To serve: Transfer the warmed cocktail to a carafe, then pour it from the carafe into the ice bowl; the warmed cocktail will melt it through. Use a spoon to break the bowl into the components below. Stir to mix and enjoy.

Tomato Water

Makes 4 cups (1 L)

2 lb (907 g) ripe heirloom tomatoes, halved

In a food processor, pulse the tomatoes until evenly chopped. Transfer the chopped tomatoes to a cheesecloth-lined chinois set over a large bowl and let sit in the fridge overnight to collect the tomato water. Tomato water is extremely perishable, so store only what you need in an airtight container in the fridge for up to 3 days. Store the remaining tomato water in the freezer for up to 1 month.

Pickled Beet Brunoise

Makes approximately ¾ cup (180 ml)

¾ cup (180 ml) beet brine, strained from pickled beets
2 g agar

In a small pot over medium heat, bring the beet brine and agar to 203°F (95°C) and let simmer for just 5 seconds, to activate the agar. Using a chinois, strain into a third pan. Let set on a flat surface at room temperature until it forms a gel. Remove from the sheet and cut into ¼ inch (6 mm) cubes (called "brunoise"). Store in an airtight container in the fridge for up to 4 days.

Tomato Ice Bowl

Makes 4 bowls

12 oz (350 ml) ladle
1 cup (250 ml) Tomato Water (see left)
2 cups (370 g) dry ice pellets (see p. 6)

Pour the tomato water into a medium bowl.

In a food processor, crush the dry ice pellets into a very fine dust, until the pieces are no larger than pea-sized, approximately 30 seconds. Fill the ladle with the pulverized dry ice to freeze it. Slowly dip the ladle into the tomato water for 1 second to coat the bowl of the ladle up to ¾ inch (2 cm) from the lip, then remove and hold in the air to allow the tomato water to freeze on it. Dip and freeze six more times.

Empty the dry ice from the ladle into a bowl and fill the ladle with warm water. Working over the dry ice, very carefully use your fingers to evenly press on the edges of the ice bowl until it pops off into the bowl. Repeat this process with the remaining tomato water. You should have enough to make four ice bowls.

Store in an airtight container in the freezer for up to 4 days.

Clamato Snow

Makes approximately 1½ cups (375 ml)

1 cup (250 ml) Clamato
3½ oz (105 ml) water
2 cups (370 g) dry ice pellets (see p. 6)

In a measuring container, combine the Clamato and water.

In a food processor, crush the dry ice pellets into a very fine dust, until the pieces are no larger than pea-sized, approximately 30 seconds. With the food processor on medium speed, slowly pour in the Clamato mixture. Store the snow in an airtight container in the freezer for up to 3 days.

Deep-Fried Capers

Makes ¼ cup (60 ml)

8 cups (2 L) canola oil
¼ cup (60 ml) capers

In a medium pot over medium heat, bring the canola oil to 350°F (180°C). Add the capers and stir occasionally until they bloom and are golden, approximately 3 minutes. Using a slotted spoon, transfer the capers to a paper towel to dry. Store in an airtight container (on a fresh piece of paper towel, to absorb residual oil) at room temperature for up to 3 days.

Celery Snow

Makes approximately 1¾ cups (430 ml)

7½ oz (225 ml) fresh celery juice
6 oz (180 ml) water
2 cups (370 g) dry ice pellets (see p. 6)

In a measuring container, combine the celery juice and water.

In a food processor, crush the dry ice pellets into a very fine dust, until the pieces are no larger than pea-sized, approximately 30 seconds. With the food processor on medium speed, slowly pour in the celery mixture. Turn off the food processor as soon as you have finished pouring. Store the snow in an airtight container in the freezer for up to 3 days.

Inspired Sips

These savory cocktails follow Heirloom Caesar's lead with slight umami notes for an intriguing, lingering mouthful.

Heirloom Old-Fashioned

Makes 1 • Glass: Old-fashioned

2 oz (60 ml) London dry gin
½ oz (15 ml) Tomato Water (p. 102)
¼ oz (8 ml) Star Anise Syrup (p. 21)
¼ oz (8 ml) Toasted Chamomile and Saffron Bitters (p. 17)
3 orange peels
King ice cube

Put the gin, tomato water, syrup, bitters, and 2 orange peels into an old-fashioned glass. Muddle the orange peels. Add the king ice cube and stir to chill, approximately three rotations. Garnish the cocktail with a flamed orange peel: Hold a lit match beside the cocktail in one hand and the remaining orange peel in the other. Squeeze the peel between your index finger and thumb toward the match, igniting oils from the peel. Discard the peel. Serve.

Celery and Rose Julep

Makes 1 • Glass: Julep cup

¼ cup (60 ml) Celery Snow (p. 103)
2 oz (60 ml) bourbon
¾ oz (23 ml) Thyme Syrup (p. 21)
¼ oz (8 ml) Amaro Montenegro
Grapefruit peel, to garnish
3 stems fresh mint, to garnish
Rose water, to garnish

Fill a julep cup halfway with celery snow, then finish filling with crushed ice. Pour the bourbon, syrup, and amaro into a mixing glass. Fill the mixing glass with ice and stir to chill, approximately three rotations. Using a Hawthorne strainer, fine-strain into the julep cup. Gently squeeze the peel between your index finger and thumb to extract the oils into the cocktail. Discard the peel. Garnish with the fresh mint and a spritz of rose water. Serve.

Strawberry and Tomato Negroni

Makes 1 • Glass: Double old-fashioned

6 king cube molds

4 cups (1 L) Tomato Water (p. 102)
1 oz (30 ml) Strawberry Gin (p. 18)
1 oz (30 ml) Campari
1 oz (30 ml) Madeira
Orange peel, to garnish

Fill the king cube molds with tomato water and freeze. Remove the frozen tomato king cubes from the molds and place one in a double old-fashioned glass.

Pour the strawberry gin, Campari, and Madeira into a mixing glass. Fill the mixing glass with ice and stir to chill, approximately three rotations. Using a Hawthorne strainer, fine-strain over the tomato king cube. Gently squeeze the peel between your index finger and thumb to extract the oils into the cocktail. Place the orange peel on the king cube as garnish. Serve.

Pictured opposite: Strawberry and Tomato Negroni

Piña Colada

Inspired by the aroma combination of cedar, ginger, and coconut (the latter common in Thai cuisine), this cocktail utilizes our full arsenal of techniques at BarChef to manipulate the textures of liquid and alcohol in a true representation of modernism in cocktails. With the introduction of Pure-Cote B790, a corn-based starch used for creating paper-like textures out of many ingredients, we were able to create roasted pineapple paper as well as coconut paper. The pellet ice provides insulation, keeping the service piece cold, to give longevity to the ice components inside, something always to be mindful of. This is one of my current favorites in the program, as it's also a collaborative effort with Frankie Solarik Holdings' Beverage Director, Gianluca Passuello, who worked with me on this recipe to create the delicious clarified cocktail served in this composition.

Makes 1
Glass: Double old-fashioned

PLATING

- Crushed ice
- 14-inch (35 cm) diameter, 4-inch (10 cm) deep ceramic bowl
- 8-inch (20 cm) diameter, 1¼-inch (3 cm) deep ceramic bowl
- Styrofoam container

- 3 cups (555 g) pellet ice
- 4 cups (1 L) liquid nitrogen
- 1 lime segment
- ½ oz (15 ml) Coconut and Cedar Fluid Gel (p. 109)
- 1 Piña Colada Sherbet Cube (p. 109)
- ½ oz (15 ml) Maraschino and Rose Fluid Gel (p. 109)
- 1 heaping tbsp (20 ml) Pineapple and Ginger Ice Gel Pearls (p. 109)
- 1 Coconut Paper Disk (p. 110)
- 1 lime peel
- ½ cup (125 ml) edible flower petals
- 1 piece Roasted Pineapple Paper (p. 108)
- 3 oz (90 ml) Clarified Piña Colada (p. 108)

To plate: Fill the 14-inch (35 cm) bowl with crushed ice. Place the 8-inch (20 cm) bowl atop the ice in the center of the large bowl. Surround the small bowl with the pellet ice.

Fill a Styrofoam container with the liquid nitrogen. Using a steel ladle, submerge the lime segment in the liquid nitrogen to freeze. Transfer to a mortar and use the pestle to crush the segment to separate the lime into individual cells.

Squeeze a dot of coconut and cedar gel in the center of the small bowl. Place the sherbet cube on the gel to adhere it in place. Surround the cube with the lime cells.

Approximately 3 inches (8 cm) away from the sherbet cube, squeeze 6 drops of coconut cedar gel in a circle, leaving space between each. Squeeze 6 dots of the maraschino rose gel in the spaces. Arrange the pearls around the sherbet cube.

Place the coconut paper disk on top of the sherbet cube. In the center of the disk, squeeze 1 dot of coconut cedar gel to stabilize the roasted pineapple paper.

Using a Microplane, grate lime peel onto the disk, then dust it with edible flower petals. Place the pineapple paper on the gel on the disk.

To serve: Pour the clarified piña colada into a double old-fashioned glass over ice. Enjoy by accompanying each sip of the cocktail with a spoonful of a variety of the edible components.

Clarified Piña Colada

Makes approximately 17 oz (500 ml) clarified cocktail

3¾ oz (110 ml) 3.25% milk
2½ oz (75 ml) coconut milk
5 oz (150 ml) white rum
3¾ oz (110 ml) coconut rum
3¾ oz (110 ml) Ginger Syrup (p. 20)
3¾ oz (110 ml) pineapple juice
¾ oz (23 ml) fresh lime juice

Pour the 3.25% milk and coconut milk into a measuring container. Pour the remaining ingredients in another measuring container, to make the cocktail base. Slowly pour the milk mixture into the cocktail base. This will cause the proteins to curdle and filter out the impurities, resulting in a clear liquid. Using a spoon, give the mixture a couple of delicate stirs.

Chill in the fridge overnight.

The next day, you should see curdles of milk protein. Using a chinois lined with two cheesecloths, strain the mixture into a measuring container. You will get an opaque mixture. Strain again into another measuring container, using the same cheesecloth; this liquid should be clear.

Store in an airtight container in the fridge for up to 2 weeks. This cocktail is also amazing enjoyed on its own on a hot summer's day.

Roasted Pineapple Paper

Makes approximately 15 pieces

Dehydrator
Atomizer with water

3 cups (750 ml) pineapple juice
1 oz (28 g) Pure-Cote B790
1 g citric acid
0.3 g xanthan gum

To clarify the pineapple juice, let it sit in a container in the fridge overnight. The next day, once the juice has settled, carefully and slowly pour the "clarified" juice into a measuring container to measure out 1 cup (250 ml) clarified juice.

Line a large baking sheet with a Silpat.

Put the clarified juice, Pure-Cote, citric acid, and xanthan gum into a measuring container. Using an immersion blender, gently blitz to dissolve the Pure-Cote, citric acid, and xanthan.

In a small pot over low heat, bring the mixture to 185°F (85°C) and let simmer for 3 seconds. Using a tablespoon, carefully remove the froth from the surface. Pour the liquid onto the prepared baking sheet while agitating it to achieve a clear liquid. Gently shake the sheet to spread the pineapple mixture into a thin, even layer, ideally ⅒-inch (2.5 mm) deep. Let sit on a flat surface at room temperature overnight, until completely dry.

Preheat the oven to 185°F (85°C). Roast the pineapple mixture for 15 minutes, or until slightly browned.

Meanwhile, preheat the dehydrator to 130°F (54°C).

Remove the pineapple paper from the oven and let cool. Use an atomizer to carefully spritz it with water to create a pliable texture. Carefully peel off small pieces to make a crinkled paper effect, and so that the paper crumples into a rough shape slightly smaller than a golf ball.

Place the crumpled paper on a tray in the dehydrator and dehydrate for 6 hours, or until crispy. Store in an airtight container at room temperature for up to 5 days.

Coconut and Cedar Fluid Gel

Makes approximately 1 cup (250 ml)

- 6¾ oz (200 ml) coconut milk
- 2½ oz (75 ml) coconut rum
- 1¾ oz (50 ml) Vanilla Syrup (p. 21)
- ¼ tsp (1 tsp) food-grade Virginia cedarwood essential oil
- 3 g agar

In a medium pot over medium heat, bring the coconut milk, rum, and syrup to 195°F (91°C). Pour into a steel container and let set on a flat surface at room temperature until firm to the touch, approximately 1 hour. Add the cedar essential oil. Using an immersion blender, blend the mixture until smooth. Store in a squeeze bottle in the fridge for up to 3 days.

Piña Colada Sherbet Cubes

Makes approximately 3 cups (750 ml) sherbet

King cube molds

- 17½ oz (500 g) peeled and chopped pineapple chunks
- 5 oz (150 ml) coconut milk
- 4½ oz (135 ml) 35% heavy cream
- 4½ oz (135 ml) coconut rum
- ½ cup (125 ml) corn syrup
- 2 oz (60 ml) fresh ginger juice
- 1¾ oz (50 ml) pineapple juice
- 1 oz (30 ml) fresh lime juice
- ¼ tsp (1 tsp) cedar oil

In a blender, blend all the ingredients together, making sure the pineapple chunks are fully blended in. Pour into the king cube molds and freeze until solid, for 6 hours. Store the frozen sherbet cubes in an airtight container in the freezer for up to 3 days.

Maraschino and Rose Fluid Gel

Makes approximately 1 cup (250 ml)

- 5 oz (150 ml) maraschino syrup
- 1¾ oz (50 ml) water
- 1 oz (30 ml) rose water
- 3 g agar

In a medium pot over medium heat, bring all the ingredients to 198°F (92°C). Pour into a steel container and let set on a flat surface at room temperature until firm to the touch, approximately 1 hour. Using an immersion blender, blend the mixture until smooth. Store in a squeeze bottle in the fridge for up to 3 days.

Pineapple and Ginger Ice Gel Pearls

Makes approximately 1 cup (250 ml) pearls

Styrofoam container

- 1 cup (250 ml) pineapple juice
- 2 oz (60 ml) pineapple liqueur
- 1 oz (30 ml) fresh ginger juice
- 3 g agar
- 8 cups (2 L) liquid nitrogen

In a small pot over low heat, bring the pineapple juice, pineapple liqueur, ginger juice, and agar to 198°F (92°C) and let simmer for 3 seconds, to activate the agar. Remove from the heat and let cool slightly. Fill a Styrofoam container with the liquid nitrogen. Transfer the pineapple mixture to a squeeze bottle and slowly squeeze drops into the liquid nitrogen to poach into pearls, using up all the mixture. Using a ladle, transfer the pearls to an airtight container. Store in the freezer for up to 3 days.

Coconut Paper Disks

Makes approximately 10

Dehydrator
2½-inch (6 cm) ring mold

6¾ oz (200 ml) coconut milk
1¾ oz (50 ml) coconut rum
1 oz (28 g) Pure-Cote B790
5 g white sugar
0.2 g xanthan gum

Line a large baking sheet with a Silpat.

In a small pot over medium heat, bring all the ingredients to a simmer, stirring to dissolve the Pure-Cote completely.

Using a chinois, fine-strain the mixture onto the prepared baking sheet. Gently shake the sheet to distribute the coconut mixture into a thin, even layer, ideally 1⁄10 inch (2.5 mm) deep. Let sit overnight at room temperature until partially dry.

The next day, preheat the dehydrator to 203°F (95°C). Place the baking sheet upside down on a cutting board and carefully remove the sheet of coconut paper from the Silpat. Settle the ring mold into the paper, then use a sharp paring knife to cut around the mold. Remove the disk. Repeat until you have 10 disks. Transfer the disks to the dehydrator and dehydrate until crisp, approximately 2 hours. Store in an airtight container at room temperature for up to 2 days.

Inspired Sips

Sweetness is at play with herby and floral brightness here, jumping off of the Piña Colada's complexity.

Gin and Violet Sour

Makes 1 • Glass: Coupe

1 oz (30 ml) Vanilla Syrup (p. 21)
4 g lavender sugar, to rim
1½ oz (45 ml) London dry gin
1 oz (30 ml) fresh lemon juice
½ oz (15 ml) violet liqueur
1 egg white
Grapefruit peel, to garnish

Pour ½ oz (15 ml) vanilla syrup onto a plate. Pour the lavender sugar onto a second plate. Dip the rim of the coupe glass at a 45-degree angle into the syrup, rotating to cover the entire rim of the glass. Use the same method to coat the rim of the glass with the lavender sugar.

Put the remaining ½ oz (15 ml) syrup, the gin, lemon juice, violet liqueur, and egg white into a shaker. Dry shake to aerate the egg white. Fill the shaker with ice and shake for 2 seconds to chill. Using a Hawthorne strainer, fine-strain into a coupe glass. Gently squeeze the peel between your index finger and thumb to extract the oils into the cocktail. Discard the peel. Serve.

Spruce Tip Rose

Makes 1 • Glass: Wine

1½ oz (45 ml) Spruce Tip Gin (p. 18)
½ oz (15 ml) late harvest Vidal
½ oz (15 ml) St-Germain
¼ oz (8 ml) Campari
¼ oz (8 ml) Ginger Syrup (p. 20)
Red grapefruit peel
Mint sprig, to garnish

Put all the ingredients except the mint into a mixing glass. Muddle the grapefruit peel. Fill the mixing glass with ice and stir to chill, approximately three rotations. Using a Hawthorne strainer, fine-strain into a wine glass. Garnish with the mint. Serve.

Vanilla Basil

Makes 1 • Glass: Collins

3 oz (90 ml) tonic water
1 oz (30 ml) London dry gin
½ oz (15 ml) Campari
½ oz (15 ml) sweet vermouth
½ oz (15 ml) Vanilla Syrup (p. 21)
½ basil sprig
Grapefruit peel, to garnish

Put all the ingredients except the grapefruit peel into a mixing glass. Muddle the basil. Fill the mixing glass with ice and stir to chill, approximately three rotations. Using a Hawthorne strainer, fine-strain over ice cubes into a collins glass. Gently squeeze the peel between your index finger and thumb to extract the oils into the cocktail. Discard the peel. Serve.

Pictured opposite: Spruce Tip Rose

Oceanic

Makes 1
Glass: Tall glass bowl, approximately 6 × 4 inches (15 × 10 cm) (the ice bowl must be able to sit on its mouth)

A cocktail inspired by the essence of the ocean and the color tones of the tropical Caribbean Sea—turquoise and deep aqua blues, the whites of waves, and the bright green of vibrant corals and algae. Most importantly, it also captures the tone of one of my favorite scents, Tom Ford's Soleil Blanc. This cocktail's flavor profile and aroma are built around the base notes of this scent. I found the fragrance's evocative pastel and cream aromas so intriguing, with its slight hints of cedar and confectionary florals and accents of citrus, that I felt it just needed to be captured in a modernist cocktail. There are a lot of progressive techniques at play here, including the multicolored transitional gel that represents the curling wave of the sea. Another example of curating ingredients that pair well together to create a truly wonderful composition.

COCKTAIL

Serving carafe

- 3 oz (90 ml) White Chocolate Water (p. 49)
- 2 oz (60 ml) coconut rum
- ⅛ oz (4 ml) Lavander Maraschino (p. 19)

PLATING

- 3 tbsp (45 ml) Violet Cream Snow (p. 116)
- 3 tbsp (45 ml) Pear and Pastis Snow (p. 116)
- ½ oz (15 ml) Blue Curaçao Fluid Gel (p. 116)
- 6 micro tarragon sprigs
- 1 White Chocolate and Cedar Bowl (p. 116)
- 1 Curaçao and Elderflower Cream Wave (p. 117)
- ½ oz (15 ml) Violet and Almond Orgeat Fluid Gel (p. 28)
- 6 fronds micro cilantro
- 1 tbsp (15 ml) Elderflower Air (p. 117)

To compose the cocktail: In a small pot over low heat, warm the white chocolate water, coconut rum, and lavender maraschino while you plate the remaining components.

To plate: Place the violet snow in the glass bowl. Place the pear snow in the bowl beside the violet cream snow.

Squeeze 6 drops of the curaçao gel throughout the snow. Garnish each with a sprig of micro tarragon.

Place the white chocolate and cedar bowl atop the mouth of the tall glass bowl. Carefully form the curaçao and elderflower cream wave with your fingers to create a coil. Place the coil in the ice bowl.

Squeeze 6 drops of the violet and almond orgeat gel into the ice bowl and garnish each with a cilantro sprout. Place the elderflower air by the wave.

To serve: Transfer the warmed cocktail to a carafe, then pour it from the carafe over the components in the ice bowl.

Violet Cream Snow

Makes approximately 2 cups (500 ml)

- 6¾ oz (200 ml) 10% cream
- 5 oz (150 ml) violet liqueur
- 1 drop organic food-grade red grapefruit essential oil
- 1¾ oz (50 ml) water
- 2 cups (370 g) dry ice pellets (see p. 6)

In a measuring container, combine the cream, violet liqueur, essential oil, and water.

In a food processor, crush the dry ice pellets into a very fine dust, until the pieces are no larger than pea-sized, approximately 30 seconds. With the food processor on medium speed, slowly pour in the violet mixture. Turn off the food processor as soon as you have finished pouring. Store the snow in the freezer in an airtight container for up to 3 days.

Pear and Pastis Snow

Makes approximately 2 cups (500 ml)

- 1 cup (250 ml) water
- 3½ oz (105 ml) pear eau-de-vie
- 1¾ oz (50 ml) pastis
- 2 cups (370 g) dry ice pellets (see p. 6)

In a measuring container, combine the water, eau-de-vie, and pastis.

In a food processor, crush the dry ice pellets into a very fine dust, until the pieces are no larger than pea-sized, approximately 30 seconds. With the food processor on medium speed, slowly pour in the reserved pear mixture. Turn off the food processor as soon as you have finished pouring. Store the snow in the freezer in an airtight container for up to 3 days.

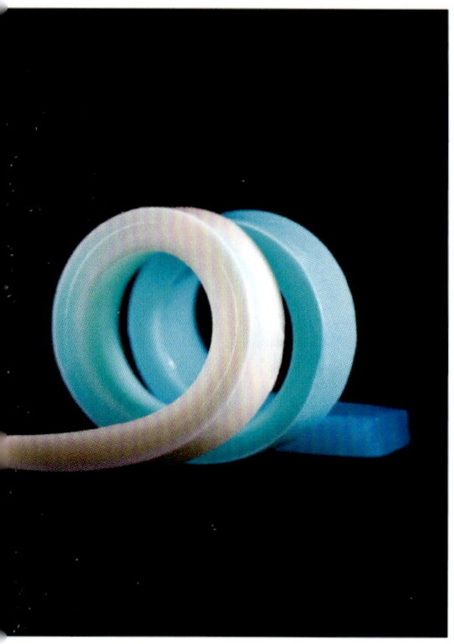

Blue Curaçao Fluid Gel

Makes approximately 1 cup (250 ml)

- 3½ oz (105 ml) blue curaçao
- 3½ oz (105 ml) water
- 3 g agar

In a small pot over medium heat, bring all the ingredients to 195°F (91°C) and let simmer for 3 seconds, to activate the agar. Pour into a steel container and let set on a flat surface at room temperature until firm to the touch, approximately 1 hour. Using an immersion blender, blend the mixture until smooth. Store in a squeeze bottle in the fridge for up to 3 days.

White Chocolate and Cedar Bowls

Makes approximately 6

12 oz (350 ml) steel ladle

- 2 cups (500 ml) White Chocolate Water (p. 49)
- 10 drops (1.25 ml) organic food-grade Virginia cedar essential oil
- 2 cups (370 g) dry ice pellets (see p. 6)

In a small bowl, stir together the white chocolate water and cedar essential oil.

In a food processor, pulverize the dry ice pellets into a fine sand texture. Fill the ladle with the pulverized dry ice to freeze the ladle. Slowly dip the ladle into the chocolate mixture for 1 second to coat the outside of the ladle up to ¾ inch (2 cm) from the lip, then remove the ladle and hold in the air to allow the water to freeze on it. Once frozen, resubmerge the ladle to create another layer of ice level with the first layer. Repeat the process until the ice bowl is approximately ⅓ inch (7.5 mm) thick.

Pour out the dry ice from the ladle and fill the ladle with tepid water, so that it is warm enough to use your fingers to slowly remove the ice bowl. Repeat this entire process with the remaining chocolate mixture. You should have enough to make six ice bowls. Store in an airtight container in the freezer for up to 3 days.

Elderflower Air

Makes approximately 2 cups (500 ml)

- 2 cups (500 ml) elderflower soda (I prefer Bottle Green)
- 2 g soy lecithin

In a measuring container and using an immersion blender, blend the elderflower soda and soy lecithin until lecithin is dissolved. Blend the surface until bubbles form. Store in an airtight container in the fridge for up to 2 days.

Curaçao and Elderflower Cream Waves

Makes approximately 10

- ½ cup (125 ml) 10% cream
- 2½ oz (75 ml) St-Germain
- 6 sheets gelatin
- 1 g gellan gum
- 4¼ oz (125 ml) blue curaçao
- 5 tbsp (75 ml) water

In a small pot over medium heat, heat the cream and St-Germain at a gentle simmer. Add 3½ sheets gelatin and 0.5g gellan gum. Bring the mixture to 200°F (93°C) and let simmer for 3 seconds, stirring until the gelatin is fully dissolved. Remove from the heat and set aside.

In another small pot over medium heat, bring the curaçao, water, and the remaining 2½ sheets gelatin and 0.5 g gellan gum to 195°F (91°C) and let simmer for 3 seconds, stirring until the gelatin is fully dissolved.

Slowly pour each mixture into opposite sides of a shallow steel double third pan on a flat surface. The mixtures will meet to create a gradual two-tone base. Place in the fridge on a flat surface for 1 hour or until fully set and firm to the touch. Carefully transfer the gel to a clean work surface. Square up any rounded corners, then slice the gel into ten ½-inch (1 cm) wide ribbons. Store in a parchment paper-lined airtight container in the fridge for up to 3 days.

Inspired Sips

These Oceanic-inspired sips fascinate the senses with lavender and elderflower notes.

Lavender and Basil

Makes 1 • Glass: Coupe

1½ oz (45 ml) London dry gin
¾ oz (23 ml) fresh lemon juice
¼ oz (8 ml) Lavender Maraschino (p. 19)
¼ oz (8 ml) Aperol
⅛ oz (4 ml) pastis
1 egg white
Grapefruit peel, to garnish

Put all the ingredients except the grapefruit peel into a shaker and dry shake to aerate the egg white. Fill the shaker with ice and shake for 2 seconds to chill. Using a Hawthorne strainer, fine-strain into a coupe glass. Gently squeeze the peel between your index finger and thumb to extract the oils into the cocktail. Discard the peel. Serve.

Pineapple Cream Daiquiri

Makes 1 • Glass: Coupe

1¾ oz (50 ml) Sailor Jerry spiced rum
1 oz (30 ml) pineapple juice
½ oz (15 ml) fresh lemon juice
½ oz (15 ml) 10% cream
¼ oz (8 ml) Lavender Maraschino (p. 19)
Absinthe, in an atomizer
Grapefruit peel, to garnish
Edible flower petals, to garnish

Put the rum, pineapple juice, lemon juice, cream, and maraschino into a shaker. Fill the shaker with ice and shake for 2 seconds to chill. Using a Hawthorne strainer, fine-strain into a coupe glass. Garnish with flamed atomized essence of absinthe: Hold a lighter in front of the nozzle of the atomizer of absinthe, and spritz twice through the flame of the lighter over the cocktail. Gently squeeze the peel between your index finger and thumb to extract the oils into the cocktail. Discard the peel. Garnish by floating a few edible flower petals on the cocktail. Serve.

Spruce and Elderflower Spritz

Makes 1 • Glass: Collins

1¾ oz (50 ml) Spruce Tip Gin (p. 18)
1 oz (30 ml) Thyme Syrup (p. 21)
¼ oz (8 ml) Green Cardamom Maraschino (p. 19)
⅛ oz (4 ml) pastis
3 oz (90 ml) elderflower presse
1 tarragon sprig
2 tbsp (30 ml) Elderflower Air (p. 117)
Red grapefruit peel, to garnish

Pour the gin, syrup, maraschino, and pastis into a collins glass. Fill the glass with ice, add the elderflower presse, and stir to incorporate. Garnish with the tarragon in the glass and the elderflower air on top of the cocktail. Gently squeeze the peel between your index finger and thumb to extract the oils onto the cocktail. Discard the peel. Serve.

Pictured opposite: Pineapple Cream Daiquiri

AUTUMN

From a flavor and composition standpoint, autumn is easily one of the most evocative seasons. It is rife with opportunities to showcase the typical fall flavors in your compositions. For example, the colors naturally associated with autumn, and the ones I generally see in my home province of Ontario, are oranges, browns, reds, and forest greens. When considering flavors that are associated with these colors, browns could be represented by chocolate, bourbon, vanilla, maple, cinnamon, or star anise; orange by notes of apricot, actual oranges, or pumpkin; red by apple, cranberry, or pomegranate; forest greens by rosemary, Chartreuse, pear, mint, or thyme. Flavor pairing can often be done based on the colors of those ingredients and which of those colors work well together—those colors can then be "translated" back to their traditionally associated flavors. This approach has definitely been a valuable tool for me over the years when composing flavor combinations.

The Apricot

This cocktail celebrates the curiously autumnal profile of a classic summer fruit. Orange and red are what I consider the quintessential colors of autumn, and so I drew from the flavors associated with these colors. My intention with this composition was to create techniques that would accurately articulate the original flavor of the fruit within unexpected textures. Specifically, the effect of dehydrating the apricot to transfer its pure flavor to the sugar, which is then used to form the meringues. The experience of consuming ends with the surprising textures of the meringue's crunch —so dominantly flavored of apricot—and the resulting dragon's breath. The use of liquid nitrogen allows for another exciting textural surprise, while continuing to bring out flavors on the palate, and is a captivating visual presentation. The abstract service piece resembles a firework or perhaps a tree of sorts, the apricot meringues seemingly growing on it.

Makes 1
Glass: Tulip Burgundy

PLATING

- Styrofoam container
- Pronged service piece

- 10 Apricot Meringue Demispheres (p. 126)
- 2 oz (60 ml) Madeira and Maple Fluid Gel (p. 126)
- 8 cups (2 L) liquid nitrogen
- 5 mint leaves
- Orange peel, to garnish

COCKTAIL

- 1 oz (30 ml) Islay Scotch
- ¾ oz (23 ml) Apricot Brandy (p. 18)
- ½ oz (15 ml) amaretto
- ¼ oz (8 ml) Madeira
- ¼ oz (8 ml) Rosemary Syrup (p. 21)
- ¼ oz (8 ml) Toasted Chamomile and Saffron Bitters (p. 17)

To plate: Place 5 demispheres on a cutting board and add a small dollop of the gel onto the flat surface of each. Using the remaining demispheres, create whole spheres: place the flat side of an unadorned demisphere onto the gelled side of an adorned demisphere. The gel should stick them together. Repeat with the remaining demispheres.

Fill a Styrofoam container with the liquid nitrogen. Using a spoon, carefully place the 5 completed spheres in liquid nitrogen for 2 minutes to poach, then remove; they should feel cool. Put a small dollop of the gel on each and adhere a mint leaf to each, to resemble leaves. Arrange the spheres on the prongs of the service piece.

Hold the orange peel between your index finger and thumb and squeeze overtop the service piece to extract oils.

To compose the cocktail: Pour all the cocktail ingredients into a mixing glass. Fill the glass with ice and stir to chill, approximately three rotations. Using a Hawthorne strainer, strain into a tulip Burgundy glass. Place the glass to the right of the service piece.

To serve: Eat 1 meringue before taking a sip of the cocktail, to achieve a "dragon's breath" effect.

Apricot Sugar

Makes approximately 2 cups (490 g)

Dehydrator

2 cups (410 g) white sugar

3½ oz (100 g) dried apricots

In a food processor, blend the sugar and apricots thoroughly, until you achieve a bright orange color and the apricots are evenly distributed and the texture of sand.

Preheat the dehydrator to 165°F (74°C). Spead the apricot sugar on a tray and dehydrate for 5 hours. If it's not fully dry after 5 hours, break the sugar into small pieces and return to the dehydrator for another 1 hour, or until fully dry.

In the food processor, blend the dehydrated apricot sugar until fine. Store in an airtight container at room temperature for up to 5 days.

Apricot Meringue Demispheres

Makes approximately 40

Dehydrator
Forty 1-inch demisphere molds
Styrofoam container

2 egg whites, room temperature

3 tbsp (40 g) Apricot Sugar (see above)

8 cups (2 L) liquid nitrogen

Preheat the dehydrator to 165°F (74°C).

In a medium stainless-steel bowl and using a hand mixer, whip the egg whites. With the blender running, very slowly add the apricot sugar, continuing to whip until stiff peaks form. Using an offset spatula, fill the demisphere molds with the mixture, gently applying pressure to make sure the molds are evenly filled.

Fill a Styrofoam container with the liquid nitrogen. Submerge the filled molds in the liquid nitrogen for 15 seconds, or until frozen. Carefully remove the frozen demispheres from their molds and place on trays in a dehydrator, making sure they aren't touching each other. Dehydrate for approximately 5½ hours, or until color darkens. Store in an airtight container at room temperature for up to 5 days.

Maple and Madeira Fluid Gel

Makes approximately 10 oz (300 ml)

3½ oz (105 ml) amaretto

3½ oz (105 ml) Madeira

1¾ oz (50 ml) maple syrup

1¾ oz (50 ml) water

3 g agar

In a medium pot over medium heat, bring all the ingredients to 192°F (89°C) and simmer for 3 minutes, to activate the agar. Pour the mixture into a plastic container and let set on a flat surface at room temperature until firm to the touch, approximately 30 minutes. Using an immersion blender, blend the mixture until smooth. Store in a squeeze bottle in the fridge for up to 3 days.

Inspired Sips

Warm spices and syrups play with rich spirits here with a nod to The Apricot.

Harvest Spritz

Makes 1 • Glass: White wine

26 oz (750 ml) vodka
7 tbsp (104 g) Apricot Sugar (p. 126)
Soda water
Mint crown, to garnish

To make apricot liqueur, put the vodka and apricot sugar in a 34 oz (1 L) mason jar. Stir until the sugar is dissolved, then let sit for 2 hours. Using a chinois, strain into an airtight container. Store at room temperature in low light. The liqueur will last indefinitely.

Into a white wine glass filled with ice, pour 2 oz (60 ml) of the apricot liqueur, followed by a splash of soda water. Garnish with the mint. Serve.

Toasted Old-Fashioned

Makes 1 • Glass: Double old-fashioned

1¾ oz (50 ml) Canadian whisky
⅓ oz (10 ml) Toasted Chamomile and Saffron Bitters (p. 17)
¼ oz (8 ml) maple syrup
3 orange peels

Pour the whisky, bitters, and maple syrup into a double old-fashioned glass. Add 2 orange peels and muddle. Fill the glass with ice and stir to chill, approximately three rotations. Gently squeeze the peel between your index finger and thumb to extract the oils into the cocktail. Discard the peel. Serve.

Cedar and Islay

Makes 1 • Glass: Tall tulip wine

Atomizer

1 cup (250 ml) water
¼ oz (8 ml) organic food-grade Virginia cedarwood essential oil
1¼ oz (38 ml) Islay Scotch
½ oz (15 ml) amaretto
¼ oz (8 ml) sweet vermouth
¼ oz (8 ml) Star Anise Syrup (p. 21)
¼ oz (8 ml) Toasted Chamomile and Saffron Bitters (p. 17)
Grapefruit peel, to garnish

Pour the water and cedarwood oil into a lidded measuring container. Close and shake vigorously, then transfer to an atomizer. The cedar water will keep at room temperature for up to 2 weeks.

Put the Scotch, amaretto, vermouth, syrup, and bitters into a shaker. Fill the shaker with ice and stir to chill, approximately five rotations. Using a Hawthorne strainer, strain into a tall tulip wine glass. Garnish with three spritzes of the cedar water. Gently squeeze the peel between your index finger and thumb to extract the oils into the cocktail. Discard the peel. Serve.

Pictured opposite: Cedar Islay

Caraway and Rose

Makes 1
Glass: Tulip Burgundy

A cocktail inspired by the juxtaposition of beauty and dystopia. The bouquet of roses set among the charcoal in the service piece celebrates what we traditionally view as symbols of beauty (roses) growing from what seems to resemble destruction or a dystopian (charcoal) setting. The "morning dew" on the roses is achieved by the aromatics of the atomized tobacco. Visuals here represent deep and dark flavor profiles with bright accents: think roses that smell of fresh tobacco, and notes of patchouli paired with those of charred vanilla bean and fresh mint. This is a cocktail that elicits an emotional response through visual association and the misdirection of aroma.

COCKTAIL

8 oz (235 ml) steel ladle

1½ oz (45 ml) bourbon
¼ oz (8 ml) Caraway Maraschino (p. 19)
¼ oz (8 ml) Madeira
¼ oz (8 ml) Star Anise Syrup (p. 21)
¼ oz (8 ml) antiqued bitters

PLATING

Ceramic bowl
Floral foam
20 pieces wood charcoal
Eight to ten 14-inch (35 cm) stem red roses, thorns removed
Styrofoam container
8 oz (235 ml) steel ladle

5 star anise pods
1 Patchouli Bonbon (p. 132)
1 oz (30 ml) Mint and Chartreuse Fluid Gel (p. 43)
2 small mint sprigs
8 cups (2 L) liquid nitrogen
1 cup (250 ml) Vanilla Bean Charcoal Crumble (p. 132)
1 oz (30 ml) Cacao Cream and Caraway Fluid Gel (p. 62)
4 cups (1 L) Star Anise and Rose Air (p. 133)
Tobacco Perfume (p. 132)

To compose the cocktail: Pour all the cocktail ingredients into a mixing glass filled with ice. Stir to chill, approximately three rotations. Using a Hawthorne strainer, strain into a tulip Burgundy glass and set aside.

To plate: Fill the ceramic bowl with the floral foam, then arrange the charcoal throughout to hide the foam. Arrange the roses so that there are 8 to 10 roses at the back of the bowl and 1 shorter stem at the front right of the service piece.

Place the star anise on the left side of the service piece, then top with the patchouli bonbon. Garnish with a dot of the mint and Chartreuse gel and a mint sprig.

Place the crumble pieces in the bowl and garnish with 4 dots of each gel. Place 1 tsp (5 ml) star anise and rose air in the center of the crumble. Garnish with a mint sprig. Spritz the roses thoroughly with the tobacco perfume.

To serve: Place the cocktail to the right of the service piece when presenting to your guest.

Tobacco Perfume

Atomizer

4 oz (120 ml)

1 whisky-flavored cigars (I prefer Backwoods)

½ cup (125 ml) bourbon

Place the cigars and bourbon in an airtight container. Seal and set aside for 2 days to infuse. Using a chinois, fine-strain into an atomizer. Store at room temperature for up to 2 weeks.

Vanilla Bean Charcoal Crumble

Makes approximately 5 cups (1.25 L)

iSi siphon and charger (see p. 8)
Styrofoam container
4 oz (120 ml) steel ladle

2 cups (500 ml) 10% cream

3¼ oz (98 ml) Vanilla Syrup (p. 21)

⅓ oz (10 g) Vanilla Bean Charcoal (p. 169)

2 sheets gelatin

8 cups (2 L) liquid nitrogen

Prepare an ice bath.

In a small pot over low heat, bring the cream, syrup, and vanilla bean charcoal to a gentle simmer and simmer for 10 minutes. Transfer to a deep measuring container and, using an immersion blender, blend thoroughly for 20 seconds, or until the charcoal is fully incorporated. Using a chinois, fine-strain the mixture back into the pot and return to low heat. Add the gelatin and stir until it's fully dissolved. Transfer the mixture to the iSi siphon, close, and shake vigorously for 1 minute, then charge with the nitrous oxide charger. Place in the ice bath for 2 hours, or until cold to touch. Store in the fridge for up to 3 days.

Fill a Styrofoam container with the liquid nitrogen. Submerge the ladle into the liquid nitrogen and leave there until the bubbling subsides. Remove, then quickly fill the ladle with the foam in the iSi siphon. Dip into the liquid nitrogen until the foam freezes, releases from the ladle, and floats. Transfer the foam to a stainless-steel bowl and, using a spoon, crack it to create a crumble. Store in an airtight container in the freezer for up to 5 days.

Patchouli Bonbons

Makes approximately 6

Twelve 1-inch (2.5 cm) demisphere molds
Ceramic plate

1 cup (250 ml) water

⅔ cup (150 ml) Star Anise Syrup (p. 21)

2½ oz (75 ml) Patchouli Syrup (p. 21)

2½ oz (75 ml) bourbon

¾ oz (25 ml) rose water

2 g xanthan gum

7 oz (200 g) cacao butter

3½ oz (100 g) Baker's bitter chocolate

To make the filling, using an immersion blender, blend the water, syrups, bourbon, rose water, and xanthan gum until incorporated and smooth. Transfer to a third pan and let sit to remove the air bubbles, approximately 30 minutes.

Fill the demisphere molds with the filling. Freeze on a flat surface for 2 hours, until frozen solid.

Prepare a double boiler: place a stainless-steel bowl over a small pot with boiling water. Add the cacao butter and chocolate and stir frequently until melted. Remove from the heat.

Remove the frozen filling from the molds. Hold onto one piece in each hand and, using a ceramic plate, rub the flat side of a demisphere to smooth into a flat, even edge. Repeat with another demisphere. Dip a fingertip in the chocolate mixture, then spread it on the flat surface of a demisphere, to adhere the two demispheres, creating a sphere. Rub your fingers over the surface to melt any imperfections. Repeat with the remaining demispheres.

Poke a pin into a frozen sphere and submerge in the melted chocolate mixture, dipping twice to thoroughly coat, then placing in a demisphere mold. Remove the pin and use a paring knife to smooth over any excess chocolate where the pin was and to fill the hole (this avoids the interior sphere leaking once melted). Store in an airtight container in the fridge for up to 3 days.

Let sit at room temperature for 1 hour to thaw prior to serving.

Star Anise and Rose Air

Makes approximately 4 cups (1 L)

4 cups (1 L) water
1 cup (250 ml) Star Anise Syrup (p. 21)
½ cup (125 ml) rose water
3 g soy lecithin

Put the water, syrup, and rose water in a plastic bowl. Using an immersion blender, blend the surface of the mixture. Let sit for 1 minute to allow the air to stabilize. Blend the surface of liquid again until a foam forms. Let set for 1 minute, then use immediately.

Inspired Sips

The deep flavors and titular spice of Caraway and Rose live on in these simple cocktails.

Old World

Makes 1 • Glass: Tall tulip wine

1½ oz (45 ml) Vanilla Brandy (p. 18)
¼ oz (8 ml) Cocoa Bitters (p. 16)
¼ oz (8 ml) Caraway Maraschino (p. 19)
¼ oz (8 ml) Islay Scotch
¼ oz (8 ml) Madeira
¼ oz (8 ml) Patchouli Syrup (p. 21)

Pour all the ingredients into a mixing glass. Fill the mixing glass with ice and stir to chill, approximately three rotations. Using a Hawthorne strainer, fine-strain into a tall tulip wine glass. Serve.

Ontario Apple

Makes 1 • Glass: Copper mule mug

3 oz (90 ml) non-filtered organic apple juice
1½ oz (45 ml) Star Anise Syrup (p. 21)
1 oz (30 ml) brandy
2 oz (60 ml) sparkling wine
Mint crown, to garnish
Confectioners' sugar, for dusting

Pour the apple juice, syrup, and brandy into a copper mule mug. Muddle. Fill with ice and stir to chill, five rotations. Add the sparkling wine and stir again for five rotations. Garnish with the mint, then dust the mint with confectioners' sugar.

Niagara-on-the-Lake

Makes 1 • Glass: Coupe

1½ oz (45 ml) Canadian rye
½ oz (15 ml) Amaro Montenegro
½ oz (15 ml) late harvest Vidal
¼ oz (8 ml) Caraway Maraschino (p. 19)
¼ oz (8 ml) Campari
Orange peel, to garnish

Pour the rye, amaro, Vidal, maraschino, and Campari into a mixing glass. Fill with ice and stir to chill, approximately three rotations. Using a Hawthorne strainer, fine-strain into a coupe glass. Garnish the cocktail with flamed orange peel: Hold a lit match beside the cocktail in one hand and the orange peel in the other. Squeeze the peel between your index finger and thumb toward the match, igniting oils from the peel. Discard the peel. Serve.

Pictured opposite: Old World

Essence of Fall

Makes 1
Glass: Stemless goblet

A cocktail inspired by the beautiful aroma of one of my favorite seasons here in Ontario. Ontario is known for its vibrant maple trees, whose colors transition in autumn to red, orange, yellow, brown, and green; this composition utilizes these tones, also invoking the flavors associated with maple, stone fruit, evergreen, moss, and soil. The service piece for this cocktail recreates the elements of an Ontario forest floor, complete with greenery, mushrooms, fallen leaves, and bark, and pairs these visuals with aromatics that are activated tableside with the use of dry ice. This was a revolutionary cocktail for the BarChef program, as it was our first composition to conceal dry ice inside a service piece, then present and activate it at the table, engulfing the guest in a beautiful aroma of cedar, moss, and soil. (Note that this cocktail includes pure almond extract, so it's not one to serve to someone with nut allergies.)

PLATING

- 4 feet (1.2 m) chicken wire
- 8 × 8 × 3-inch (20 × 20 × 8 cm) ceramic bento box
- 3 × 3-foot (1 × 1 m) live damp sheet moss
- 8 stems myrtle
- 2 stems cedar
- 6 stems fresh orange, red, and/or yellow waxflowers
- 4 stems fresh hypericum berries
- Orange and/or red maple leaves
- 8 brown shimeji mushrooms
- 4 × 2-inch (10 × 5 cm) piece of bark
- ½ oz (15 ml) food-grade Virginia cedar oil
- 1 cup (185 g) dry ice pellets (see p. 6)
- 2 cups (500 ml) boiling water

COCKTAIL

- Serving carafe

- 1 Maple and Fernet-Branca Granita Sphere (p. 138)
- 5 tbsp (75 ml) Bitter Almond and Orange Blossom Air (p. 138)
- 2 small mint sprigs
- 1½ oz (45 ml) brandy
- ½ oz (15 ml) sweet vermouth
- ½ oz (15 ml) Rosemary Syrup (p. 21)
- ½ oz (15 ml) Balsam Fir Bitters (p. 16)

To plate: Roll up the chicken wire and place in the bento box to create a stable foundation for the florals and greens. Place the sheet moss over the chicken wire to hide it.

Arrange the myrtle and cedar in the moss throughout the service piece to resemble a forest floor, then arrange the flowers, hypericum berries, and leaves throughout. Arrange the mushrooms and bark in the moss to create a naturalistic scene.

Lift the moss and pour the oil beneath into the box, on the left and back sides of the service piece. Put the dry ice pellets on top of the oil. Cover again with the moss.

To compose the cocktail: In a stemless goblet, place the sphere, air, and mint sprigs. Place a demitasse spoon on the bento box, directly to the right of the goblet.

Pour the brandy, vermouth, syrup, and bitters into a glass serving carafe.

To serve: Pour the boiling water over the moss to activate the aromatics and dry ice. Serve with the cocktail in the carafe.

Maple and Fernet-Branca Granita Spheres

Makes 2

Two 2½-inch (6 cm) spherical ice molds

1¼ cups (310 ml) water
3¼ oz (98 ml) maple syrup
¾ oz (23 ml) Fernet-Branca

In a measuring container, stir together the water, maple syrup, and Fernet-Branca. Pour into the molds and freeze for 8 hours. To remove, rinse the sealed molds with cold water, then open the molds to remove the spheres. Store in an airtight container in the freezer for up to 5 days.

Bitter Almond and Orange Blossom Air

Makes approximately 2 cups (500 ml)

3 cups (750 ml) water
1 tbsp (12 g) white sugar
1 tsp (5 ml) orange blossom water
1 tsp (5 ml) pure almond extract
2 g soy lecithin
1 egg white

Using an immersion blender, blend the water, sugar, orange blossom water, pure almond extract, egg white, and soy lecithin until the lecithin is fully dissolved. Then blend the surface of the mixture until a foam forms. Let set for 15 seconds, then use immediately.

Inspired Sips

Woodsy notes atop deep flavors evoke the Essence of Fall's ode to the season.

Palo Santo

Makes 1 • Glass: White wine

Smoking tray
Blowtorch
Seven 2½-inch (6 cm) spherical ice molds

2 cups (500 ml) water
½ oz (14 g) Palo Santo sticks
1½ oz (45 ml) Cedar Rye (p. 19)
¼ oz (8 ml) Caraway Maraschino (p. 19)
¼ oz (8 ml) Madeira
¼ oz (8 ml) Rosemary Syrup (p. 21)
¼ oz (8 ml) Balsam Fir Bitters (p. 16)

Set up a smoking tray: Pour the water into a large container. Keep a larger container or cloche nearby. Put the Palo Santo into a steel baking tray, use a blowtorch to ignite the sticks until smoldering, then extinguish the flames, set beside the water, and enclose both with the larger container or cloche for 15 minutes. Using a chinois, fine-strain the smoked water into a measuring container. Pour 4¼ oz (125 ml) of the smoked water into four of the molds and freeze overnight.

Place the smoked ice in the Burgundy wine glass. Pour the rye, maraschino, Madeira, syrup, and bitters into a mixing glass. Fill with ice and stir to chill, approximately three rotations. Using a Hawthorne strainer, fine-strain over the ice sphere. Serve.

Warmed and Spiced Butter Scotch

Makes 1 • Glass: Teacup with saucer

1 oz (30 ml) Islay Scotch
1 oz (30 ml) Star Anise Syrup (p. 21)
½ oz (15 ml) amaretto
¼ oz (8 ml) Balsam Fir Bitters (p. 16)
1 tsp (5 ml) butter
1 pinch smoked Maldon salt
2 tbsp (30 ml) Bitter Almond and Orange Blossom Air (p. 138), to garnish
1 pinch grated cinnamon, to garnish

In a small pot, bring the Scotch, syrup, amaretto, bitters, butter, and salt to a simmer. Pour into a teacup placed on a saucer. Garnish with the bitter almond and orange blossom air and grated cinnamon. Serve.

Paris in Autumn

Makes 1 • Glass: Cocktail

1½ oz (45 ml) Vanilla Brandy (p. 18)
¼ oz (8 ml) Madeira
¼ oz (8 ml) Caraway Maraschino (p. 19)
¼ oz (8 ml) Star Anise Syrup (p. 21)
¼ oz (8 ml) Balsam Fir Bitters (p. 16)
Rosemary sprig, to garnish

Pour the brandy, Madeira, maraschino, syrup, and bitters into a shaker. Fill the shaker with ice and stir to chill, approximately three rotations. Using a Hawthorne strainer, fine-strain into a cocktail glass. Garnish with the rosemary. Serve.

Pictured opposite: Palo Santo

Vanilla Charcoal Foam

Makes approximately 2 cups (500 ml)

iSi siphon and charger (see p. 8)

2 cups (500 ml) 10% cream

3¼ oz (98 ml) Vanilla Syrup (p. 21)

¾ oz (21 g) Vanilla Bean Charcoal (p. 169)

2 sheets gelatin

Prepare an ice bath.

In a small pot over medium heat, bring the cream, syrup, and vanilla bean charcoal to a gentle simmer for 10 minutes. Pour into a deep measuring container and, using an immersion blender, blend thoroughly for 20 seconds, or until the ingredients are evenly distributed. Using a chinois, fine-strain into a measuring container. While the mixture is still warm, add the gelatin and stir until the gelatin is dissolved.

Transfer the mixture to the iSi siphon, close, and shake vigorously for 1 minute, then charge the siphon with the nitrous oxide charger. Place in the ice bath for 2 hours to chill and let the foam set. Store in the fridge for up to 5 days.

Violet au Lait Snow

Makes approximately 2 cups (500 ml)

1 cup (250 ml) water

½ cup (125 ml) violet liqueur

5 tbsp (75 ml) 2% milk

2 cups (370 g) dry ice pellets (see p. 6)

Pour the water, violet liqueur, and milk into a measuring container.

In a food processor, crush the dry ice pellets into a very fine dust, until the pieces are no larger than pea-sized, approximately 30 seconds. With the food processor on medium speed, slowly pour in the violet mixture. Turn off the food processor as soon as you've finished pouring. Store the snow in an airtight container in the freezer for up to 3 days.

Lavender Grand Marnier Fluid Gel

Makes approximately 1 cup (250 ml)

1 cup (250 ml) Lavender Grand Marnier (p. 18)

5 oz (150 ml) water

4 g agar

In a medium pot over medium heat, bring the Grand Marnier, water, and agar to 198°F (92°C) and let simmer for 3 seconds, to activate the agar. Pour into a container and let set on a flat surface at room temperature until firm to the touch, approximately 45 minutes. Using an immersion blender, blend the mixture until smooth. Store in a squeeze bottle in the fridge for up to 3 days.

Inspired Sips

Rosemary, lavender, and vanilla from Pastels of Violet settle beautifully into these evergreen cocktails.

After Eight

Makes 1 • Glass: Wine

1¾ oz (50 ml) Auchentoshan Scotch
¼ oz (8 ml) Vanilla Brandy (p. 18)
¼ oz (8 ml) sweet vermouth
¼ oz (8 ml) Rosemary Syrup (p. 21)
¼ oz (8 ml) Balsam Fir Bitters (p. 16)
1 rosemary sprig, to garnish

Put all the ingredients except the rosemary sprig into a mixing glass. Fill the mixing glass with ice and stir to chill, approximately three rotations. Using a Hawthorne strainer, fine-strain into a wine glass. Serve.

Spiced Cinnamon and Lavender Spritz

Makes 1 • Glass: Collins

1½ oz (45 ml) reposado tequila
½ oz (15 ml) Cinnamon Syrup (p. 20)
½ oz (15 ml) Amaro Montenegro
¼ oz (8 ml) Lavender Grand Marnier (p. 18)
1 oz (30 ml) ginger beer
1 oz (30 ml) sparkling wine
1 cinnamon stick, to garnish
Orange peel, to garnish

Pour the tequila, syrup, Amaro Montenegro, and Grand Marnier into a collins glass. Fill the glass with ice and stir to chill, approximately three rotations. Pour in the ginger beer and sparkling wine and lightly stir to incorporate all the ingredients. Garnish with the cinnamon stick. Gently squeeze the peel between your index finger and thumb to extract the oils into the cocktail. Discard the peel. Serve.

Pear and Rosemary

Makes 1 • Glass: Burgundy wine

1¼ oz (38 ml) mezcal
½ oz (15 ml) pear liqueur
½ oz (15 ml) Rosemary Syrup (p. 21)
¼ oz (8 ml) Balsam Fir Bitters (p. 16)
¼ oz (8 ml) Lillet Blanc
2 rosemary sprigs

Put the mezcal, pear liqueur, syrup, bitters, Lillet Blanc, and the leaves from 1 rosemary sprig into a mixing glass. Muddle. Fill the glass with ice and stir to chill, approximately five rotations. Strain into a Burgundy wine glass. Garnish with the remaining rosemary sprig. Serve.

Pictured opposite: After Eight

Clementine and Chamomile

This is a defining cocktail for the BarChef program, as it led to the creation of one of our favorite ingredients to work with that we still use to this day: toasted chamomile. In the years since, we've used it in a variety of cocktails and also in one of our most popular bitters (toasted chamomile and saffron). It came about when I was attempting to make a chamomile-flavored isomalt for this exact modernist cocktail. (Isomalt is a very stable, lightly sweet sugar that lends itself very nicely to sugar work, as it's quite resilient to warm temperatures and humidity. It's used frequently by pastry chefs in place of sugar because of this stability.) To activate the isomalt to the appropriate sugar phase, the isomalt was slowly brought up to a high temperature, at which point I added the dried chamomile flowers; they began to toast immediately. A beautiful aroma was released, and I was instantly inspired to create infusions and bitters with this wonderful ingredient. I began toasting chamomile and infusing it in a variety of spirits, which eventually led to the delicious toasted chamomile strand that features in this composition—itself a celebration of beautiful and vibrant clementine paired with almond, violet, and Campari.

Makes 1
Glass: Amber stemless coupe

PLATING

- 1 ornate amber plate
- 1 Clementine Bâtonnet (p. 154)
- 7 cilantro sprouts
- 2 tsp (10 ml) Pastis, Lemon, and Orgeat Fluid Gel (p. 155)
- 2 tsp (10 ml) Lemon and Chamomile Fluid Gel (p. 73)
- ¼ cup (60 ml) ground cacao nibs
- 1 oz (30 ml) Violet and Almond Orgeat Fluid Gel (p. 28)
- 1 tbsp (15 ml) Chamomile Tea Air (p. 155)
- 1 Toasted Chamomile Strands Sphere (p. 155)

COCKTAIL

- 1½ oz (45 ml) reposado tequila
- 1 oz (30 ml) almond orgeat
- 1 oz (30 ml) Chamomile Syrup (p. 20)
- ½ oz (15 ml) Pernod pastis
- Clementine peel
- 1 sprig thyme

To plate: On the amber plate, place the bâtonnet at the 3 o'clock position. Using a pin, poke four ¼-inch (6 mm) deep holes along the top of the bâtonnet. Place 1 cilantro sprout in each hole. Squeeze 1 dot of the pastis, lemon, and orgeat gel in between each sprout and then sporadically throughout the plate.

Squeeze 3 penny-sized dollops of lemon and chamomile gel randomly spaced on the plate. Cover each dollop with a small pile of the ground cacao, and place 1 cilantro sprout in each dollop to resemble sprouts growing from a mound of earth.

Squeeze approximately 15 dots of violet and almond orgeat gel throughout the plate.

Dollop the chamomile tea air on one end of the bâtonnet, and place the sphere at the opposite end.

To compose the cocktail: Pour the tequila, orgeat, syrup, and pastis into a shaker. Fill the shaker with ice and shake for 2 seconds to chill. Using a fine cocktail strainer, strain into a stemless coupe glass. Gently squeeze the peel between your index finger and thumb to extract the oils into the cocktail. Discard the peel. Garnish with the thyme sprig.

To serve: Sip the cocktail while alternating bites of the edible pieces.

Clementine Bâtonnets

Makes approximately 12

Juicer

1 lb (454 g) fresh clementines
5 g agar
1 oz (30 ml) Campari

Using a juicer, juice the clementines. Using a chinois, fine-strain the juice into a measuring container, until you have 1½ cups (375 ml) of juice.

In a small pot, bring the measured juice and agar to 203°F (95°C) and let simmer for 3 seconds, to activate the agar. Pour into a measuring container and stir in the Campari. Pour into a quarter pan and let set on a flat surface at room temperature until firm, approximately 30 minutes. Invert the container and, using your hands, carefully remove the set gel. Square up any rounded corners, then slice the gel into bâtonnets, each measuring 3 × ½-inch (8 × 1 cm) (you should have about 12). Store in a parchment paper–lined airtight container in the fridge for up to 5 days.

Pastis, Lemon, and Orgeat Fluid Gel

Makes approximately 1 cup (250 ml)

1 cup (250 ml) water
1 tbsp (12 g) white sugar
1 lemon peel
3½ oz (105 ml) almond orgeat
1¾ oz (50 ml) pastis
3.5 g agar

In a small pot over medium heat, bring the water, sugar, and peel to a boil, then reduce the heat to 203°F (95°C) to achieve a medium simmer for approximately 10 minutes. Remove from the heat.

Using a chinois, fine-strain the syrup into an airtight container, leaving behind 5 oz (150 ml) in the pot (see note).

Add the almond orgeat, pastis, and agar, bring to 200°F (93°C), and let simmer for just 10 seconds, to activate the agar. Pour into a steel container and let set at room temperature until firm to the touch, approximately 1 hour. Using an immersion blender, blend the mixture until smooth. Store in a squeeze bottle in the fridge for up to 5 days.

Note: The syrup will last in the fridge for up to 3 days and can be used in your favorite summer spritz cocktails. Or combine ½ oz (15 ml) with some Champagne and St-Germain and a dash of absinthe, and garnish with sliced cucumber and fresh basil, for the perfect summer spritz.

Toasted Chamomile Strands Spheres

Makes approximately 8

12 oz (350 ml) steel ladle
1 cup (78 g) isomalt
2 tsp (3 g) dried chamomile flowers

Place the isomalt in a small pot on a cold stovetop. Turn the heat to medium, constantly checking the temperature of the isomalt as it melts. Once it reaches 248°F (120°C), add the chamomile to the pot and baste with the melted isomalt. Increase the temperature of the isomalt to 275°F (135°C) and keep at that temperature for 2 minutes while basting, to allow the chamomile flowers to toast thoroughly and the flavor to infuse the isomalt. Be careful not to let it burn.

Let the isomalt reach 293°F (145°C), then, using a chinois, fine-strain into a stainless-steel bowl to cool to 275°F (135°C).

Meanwhile, place two large pots with long handles on parchment paper approximately 10 inches (25 cm) apart, their handles facing toward you.

Dip the ladle into the prepared isomalt and, from 6 inches (15 cm) above the handles, slowly string the isomalt between the handles to create isomalt strands. You'll want approximately 50 thin strands.

Using your hands, carefully slide the hardened strands from the handles. Use your hands to carefully form the strands into eight softball-sized spheres. Store in a parchment paper–lined airtight container at room temperature for up to 3 days.

Chamomile Tea Air

Makes approximately 4 cups (1 L)

4 cups (1 L) water
1 cup (30 g) dried chamomile flowers
1 tbsp (12 g) white sugar
3 g soy lecithin

In a small pot over medium heat, bring the water and chamomile to a simmer and simmer for 5 minutes. Using a chinois, fine-strain into a large bowl. Add the sugar and stir to dissolve. Add the soy lecithin. Using an immersion blender, blend the surface area of the mixture until bubbles form. Let sit for 1 minute before using immediately.

Inspired Sips

Wood and spice dominate here in homage to the toasty Clementine and Chamomile.

London Evergreen

Makes 1 • Glass: Coupe

1 ½ oz (45 ml) London dry gin
¾ oz (23 ml) almond orgeat
¼ oz (8 ml) Fernet-Branca
¼ oz (8 ml) absinthe
¼ oz (8 ml) Rosemary Syrup (p. 21)
Orange peel, to garnish

Put all the ingredients except the peel into a shaker. Fill the shaker with ice and shake for 2 seconds to chill. Using a fine cocktail strainer, strain into a coupe glass. Gently squeeze the peel between your index finger and thumb to extract the oils into the cocktail. Discard the peel. Serve.

Smooth Operator

Makes 1 • Glass: Old-fashioned

1 ½ oz (45 ml) bourbon
¼ oz (8 ml) Saffron Brandy (p. 18)
¼ oz (8 ml) Caraway Maraschino (p. 19)
¼ oz (8 ml) sherry
¼ oz (8 ml) Chamomile Syrup (p. 20)
¼ oz (8 ml) celery bitters
King ice cube
Orange peel, to garnish

Put all the ingredients except the king cube and peel into a mixing glass. Fill the mixing glass with ice and stir to chill, approximately three rotations. Using a fine cocktail strainer, strain over a king cube in an old-fashioned glass. Gently squeeze the peel between your index finger and thumb to extract the oils into the cocktail. Rest the peel on the king cube. Serve.

Cedar and Chamomile

Makes 1 • Glass: Old-fashioned

1 oz (30 ml) Cedar Rye (p. 19)
½ oz (15 ml) Madeira
½ oz (15 ml) Chamomile Syrup (p. 20)
¼ oz (10 ml) Campari
King ice cube
Red grapefruit peel, to garnish

Put all the ingredients except the king cube and peel in the mixing glass. Fill the mixing glass with ice and stir to chill, approximately three rotations. Using a Hawthorne strainer, fine-strain over a king cube in an old-fashioned glass. Gently squeeze the peel between your index finger and thumb to extract the oils into the cocktail. Rest the peel on the king cube. Serve.

Pictured opposite: London Evergreen

Crème de Blanc

Makes 1
Glass: Wide-rimmed white ceramic bowl

This warm cocktail, an adaptation of classic hot chocolate, is an expression of a monochromatic composition. White chocolate and the monochrome of white throughout the service piece via the ice components and marshmallows create a blank canvas of sorts. My intention was to remove any visual elements that are immediately tied to flavors or aromatics, so that there would be no hint to the drinker of what's to come. The pops of green from soft and herbaceous basil and from tarragon, with its slight menthol quality, provide visual distinction without revealing the cocktail's flavors. This is truly one of my favorites. The use of the monochromatic approach to color composition of this cocktail still inspires me to this day to constantly challenge the drinker.

COCKTAIL

Serving carafe

- 1½ oz (45 ml) mezcal
- ⅓ oz (10 ml) Balsam Fir Bitters (p. 16)
- ¼ oz (8 ml) Thyme Syrup (p. 21)
- ⅛ oz (4 ml) green Chartreuse
- 4 oz (120 ml) White Chocolate and Thai Chili Velouté (p. 160)

PLATING

- 1 oz (30 ml) Cacao and Thai Chili Fluid Gel (p. 162)
- 7 micro basil sprouts
- 3 tbsp (45 ml) White Chocolate and Spruce Snow (p. 162)
- 4 pieces Rose Marshmallows (p. 160)
- 1 Absinthe Ice Disk (p. 161)
- 1 Basil Liqueur Ice Disk (p. 161)
- 1 Pink Himalayan Salt Ice Disk (p. 161)
- 5 tarragon leaves
- 3 tbsp (45 ml) Green Cardamom Salt Air (p. 162)

To compose the cocktail: In a small pot, mix together the mezcal, bitters, syrup, and Chartreuse. Add the velouté and bring the mixture to a simmer over medium heat. Remove from the heat and, using an immersion blender, blend to aerate. Transfer to the serving carafe.

To plate: Squeeze 7 dots of the gel along the bowl's rim on the side closest to you, then place the micro basil in alternating dots, beginning with the furthest on the left.

Arrange the snow from the 2 o'clock to 9 o'clock position.

Line up 3 marshmallows in the snow at a 45-degree angle at the back left of the bowl, then rest 1 disk on each: Prop the absinthe ice disk up against the marshmallow on the far left. Prop the basil ice disk up against the middle marshmallow. Prop the salt ice disk up against the marshmallow on the far right.

Squeeze 2 dots of gel on the snow in front of the disks, and garnish each dot with micro basil.

Place 1 marshmallow in front of the absinthe disk, squeeze a dot of Thai gel on top, and garnish with a micro basil sprout.

Place the tarragon sprouts in the snow behind and between the disks.

Arrange the green cardamom salt air from the 3 o'clock to 8 o'clock position, making sure to not cover the micro basil.

To serve: Pour the cocktail from the carafe over the plated components. Use a spoon to enjoy each component individually or mixed together.

White Chocolate and Thai Chili Velouté

Makes approximately 3 cups (750 ml)

2 tbsp + 2 tsp (40 ml) Thai Chili Maraschino (p. 19)
1¼ oz (35 g) Baker's white chocolate
1 cup (250 ml) 2% milk
¼ cup (60 ml) 10% cream
¼ cup (60 ml) water
0.5 g xanthan gum

Put all the ingredients except the xanthan gum into a medium pot and, using an immersion blender, blend until everything is incorporated. Over low heat and stirring constantly, heat until the chocolate is fully melted, approximately 2 minutes. Be careful it doesn't burn. Remove from the heat and add the xanthan gum. Using an immersion blender, carefully blend until the xanthan gum is fully dissolved and incorporated. Store in an airtight container in the fridge for up to 2 days.

Rose Marshmallows

Makes approximately 24

Steel cannoli tube
5 sheets gelatin
1 tsp (5 ml) canola oil
1 cup (205 g) white sugar
¼ cup (60 ml) rose water
2 tbsp (30 ml) white corn syrup
0.5 g agar
2 egg whites
Confectioners' sugar, for dusting

Submerge the gelatin sheets in cold water for 30 seconds, or until they bloom, then remove from the water and wring to extract as much water as possible. Set aside.

Grease a plastic 4 × 6-inch (10 × 15 cm) container with the canola oil, then cover the inside edges with plastic wrap.

In a small pot over low heat, heat the sugar, rose water, corn syrup, and agar, stirring until the agar is dissolved. Bring the mixture to 203°F (95°C) and let simmer for 3 seconds, to activate the agar. Remove the mixture from the heat. Add the bloomed gelatin and stir until dissolved. Set aside.

Place a bowl on a kitchen towel to avoid it slipping. Add the egg whites. Using a hand blender, whip until shiny. Still whipping, slowly add the sugar-gelatin mixture and whip until fully incorporated.

Pour into the prepared pan set on a flat surface; the mixture should be approximately ¾ inch (2 cm) deep. Using a spatula, spread it to achieve a flat, even surface. Transfer to a flat surface in the fridge and let the marshmallow set until firm to the touch, approximately 2 hours.

Evenly dust a cutting board with confectioners' sugar.

Transfer the marshmallow to the dusted cutting board. Dust both sides of the marshmallow with confectioners' sugar to reduce stickiness.

Run the cannoli tube under warm water. Use the tube to cut cylinders out of the marshmallow. You should get approximately 24 marshmallows. Store in a parchment paper-lined airtight container in the fridge for up to 5 days.

Absinthe Ice Disks

Makes approximately 12

One 2-inch (5 cm) steel ring mold

1¼ cups (310 ml) water

2 oz (60 ml) Pernod absinthe

Pour the water and absinthe into a measuring container. Using an immersion blender, blend until fully combined. Pour into a three-quarter baking sheet and freeze until solid, 2 hours. Remove from the freezer and allow to temper at room temperature for 5 minutes. Use the ring mold to cut out disks. Store in an airtight container in the freezer for up to 5 days.

Basil Liqueur Ice Disks

Makes approximately 12

One 2-inch (5 cm) steel ring mold

9¼ oz (280 ml) water

3½ oz (105 ml) basil liqueur (I prefer Briottet)

Pour the water and basil liqueur into a measuring container. Using an immersion blender, blend until evenly distributed. Pour into a three-quarter baking sheet and freeze until solid, 2 hours. Remove from the freezer and allow to temper at room temperature for 5 minutes. Use the ring mold to cut out disks. Store in an airtight container in the freezer for up to 5 days.

Pink Himalayan Salt Ice Disks

Makes approximately 12

One 2-inch (5 cm) steel ring mold

1½ cups (375 ml) water

1 tsp (6 g) pink Himalayan salt

Pour the water and salt into a measuring container and stir to dissolve the salt. Pour the mixture into a three-quarter baking sheet and freeze until solid, 2 hours. Remove from the freezer and allow to temper at room temperature for 5 minutes. Use the ring mold to cut out disks. Store in an airtight container in the freezer for up to 5 days.

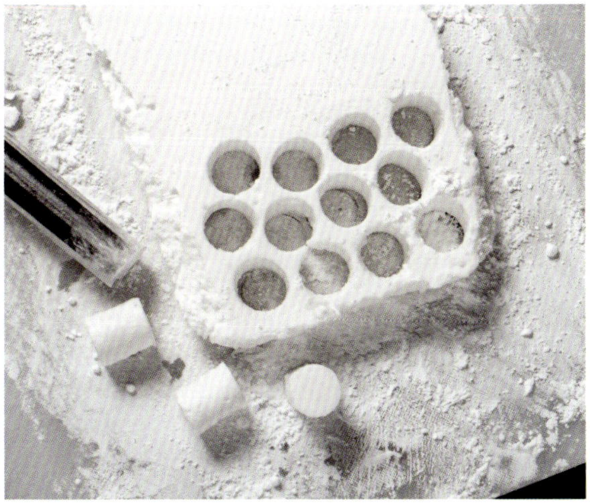

Cacao and Thai Chili Fluid Gel

Makes approximately ¾ cup (180 ml)

- 3¼ oz (98 ml) clear cacao liqueur
- 2½ oz (75 ml) Thai Chili Maraschino (p. 19)
- 3 tbsp (45 ml) water
- 3 g agar

In a medium pot over medium heat, bring the cacao liqueur, maraschino, water, and agar to 194°F (90°C), and let simmer for 3 seconds, to activate the agar. Pour into a steel container and let set on a flat surface at room temperature until firm to the touch. Transfer to a bowl and, using an immersion blender, blend the mixture until smooth. Store in a squeeze bottle in the fridge for up to 3 days.

White Chocolate and Spruce Snow

Makes approximately 2 cups (500 ml)

- 10¼ oz (305 ml) White Chocolate Water (p. 49)
- 2 oz (60 ml) Spruce Tip Gin (p. 18)
- 2 cups (370 g) dry ice pellets (see p. 6)

Pour the white chocolate water and gin into a measuring container.

In a food processor, crush the dry ice pellets into a very fine dust, until the pieces are no larger than pea-sized, approximately 30 seconds. With the food processor on medium speed, slowly pour in the gin mixture. Turn off the food processor as soon as you have finished pouring. Store the snow in an airtight container in the freezer for up to 3 days.

Green Cardamom Salt Air

Makes approximately 8 cups (2 L)

- ¼ cup (50 g) kosher salt
- 1 g seeds from green cardamom pods
- 4 cups (1 L) water
- 3 g soy lecithin

In a spice grinder, pulverize the salt and cardamom pods on high speed to a fine dust, approximately 1 minute. Using a chinois, fine-strain into an airtight container. (Store any leftover salt in an airtight container; it will last indefinitely.)

In a large bowl, combine 1 tbsp (18 g) of the green cardamom salt, the water, and soy lecithin. Using an immersion blender, blend until the lecithin is dissolved. Blend the surface to create a foam. Let set for 10 seconds, then use immediately.

Inspired Sips

Cardamom, chili, white chocolate . . . the complexity of Crème de Blanc can be spotted throughout these cocktails.

Spiced White Chocolate Ramos Fizz

Makes 1 • Glass: Collins

1 oz (30 ml) White Chocolate and Thai Chili Velouté (p. 160)
¾ oz (23 ml) fresh lemon juice
2 oz (60 ml) London dry gin
½ oz (15 ml) Vanilla Syrup (p. 21)
⅛ oz (4 ml) orange blossom water
1 egg white
2 oz (60 ml) very cold soda water

Put all the ingredients except the soda water into a shaker and shake vigorously for 20 seconds, or until the volume of the mixture has doubled. Fill the shaker with ice and shake for 10 seconds to chill. Pour the soda water into a collins glass, then carefully strain the cocktail into the glass. Serve.

Saffron and Grain

Makes 1 • Glass: Coupe

1 oz (30 ml) Amaro Montenegro
½ oz (15 ml) Canadian rye
¼ oz (8 ml) Madeira
¼ oz (8 ml) Thai Chili Maraschino (p. 19)
¼ oz (8 ml) Rosemary Syrup (p. 21)
¼ oz (8 ml) Toasted Chamomile and Saffron Bitters (p. 17)
Orange peel, to garnish

Put all the ingredients except the orange peel into a mixing glass. Fill the mixing glass with ice and stir to chill, approximately three rotations. Using a fine cocktail strainer, strain into a coupe glass. Gently squeeze the peel between your index finger and thumb to extract the oils into the cocktail. Discard the peel. Serve.

Le Paris

Makes 1 • Glass: Coupe

1½ oz (45 ml) Spruce Tip Gin (p. 18)
⅓ oz (10 ml) Thyme Syrup (p. 21)
¼ oz (8 ml) Campari
¼ oz (8 ml) St-Germain
¼ oz (8 ml) Green Cardamom Maraschino (p. 19)
¼ oz (8 ml) green Chartreuse
Lemon peel, to garnish

Put all the ingredients except the lemon peel into a mixing glass. Fill the mixing glass with ice and stir to chill, approximately three rotations. Using a fine cocktail strainer, strain into a coupe glass. Gently squeeze the peel between your index finger and thumb to extract the oils into the cocktail. Discard the peel. Serve.

Pictured opposite: Saffron and Grain

Mezcal, White Chocolate, and Eucalyptus

This cocktail evolved from the idea of having a large sprig of rosemary transform into ice, the ice slowly absorbing the flavor of the rosemary. Mimicking a snow-covered evergreen tree, this composition showcases the capabilities of flavored ices and utilizes ingredients like liquid nitrogen to create frozen components à la minute. This cocktail incorporates the smoky quality of mezcal with the wooded tones from vanilla charcoal. The cooling effect of the eucalyptus pairs seamlessly with the white chocolate's creamed and confectionary tones, similar in essence to the pairing of white chocolate and mint. While the photo on page 170 shows the elements plated freely, you will serve them within a glass.

Makes 1
Glass: Large cognac snifter

COCKTAIL

Serving carafe

- 1½ oz (45 ml) mezcal
- 1½ oz (45 ml) White Chocolate Water (p. 49)
- ½ oz (15 ml) Rosemary Syrup (p. 21)
- ¼ oz (8 ml) green Chartreuse

PLATING

Large white marble plate

- 1 White Chocolate and Pastis Bâtonnet (p. 170)
- 2 tbsp (30 ml) Vanilla Charcoal Fluid Gel (p. 169)
- 1 tbsp (15 ml) Violet Fluid Gel (p. 63)
- 1 tbsp (15 ml) Mint and Chartreuse Fluid Gel (p. 43)
- 1 tbsp (15 ml) Balsam Fir Cream Gel (p. 170)
- 1 red grapefruit, grated
- 6 thyme leaves
- 1 tsp (5 ml) Eucalyptus Air (p. 171)
- ¼ cup (60 ml) Violet Snow (p. 170)
- 2 Eucalyptus Ice Shards (p. 170)
- 1 Vanilla Charcoal Ice Shard (p. 169)
- 1 Frozen White Chocolate and Balsam Fir Rosemary Sprig (p. 171)
- 10 pieces Vanilla Bean Charcoal (p. 169)

To compose the cocktail: In a small pot over low heat, heat the mezcal, white chocolate water, syrup, and Chartreuse for the cocktail until lightly simmering. Transfer to the serving carafe. Set aside.

To plate: On the large plate, place the bâtonnet at the 6 o'clock position, then surround it with dots of various sizes of the vanilla charcoal fluid gel (reserving some for later), violet gel, and mint and Chartreuse gel, arranged in circles similar to the curves of a yin and yang symbol, and approximately ¾ inch (2 cm) in diameter (follow the recipe photo for guidance).

Place three nickel-sized dollops of the balsam fir cream gel around the bâtonnet, and garnish each with a pinch of grated grapefruit peel and 2 thyme leaves.

Place 8 or so small dots of vanilla charcoal gel along the top of the bâtonnet.

Position the eucalyptus air on the far end of the bâtonnet.

In the center of a cognac snifter, place the violet snow, eucalyptus shards, vanilla charcoal shard, and frozen rosemary sprig.

To serve: Place the cognac snifter behind the marble plate on the right side. Pour the warmed cocktail from the carafe overtop the components in the glass.

Vanilla Bean Charcoal

Makes 0.7 oz (20 g)

Blowtorch

10 vanilla beans

Using the blowtorch, char the vanilla beans until they inflate and glow, becoming very brittle embers (this allows for thorough blending and proper integration when creating the cream component later). Extinguish the flames by covering with an upside-down pan. Set aside to cool. Store in an airtight container at room temperature. The charcoal will last indefinitely.

Vanilla Charcoal Fluid Gel

Makes approximately 1 cup (250 ml)

1 cup (250 ml) 10% cream

⅓ oz (10 g) Vanilla Bean Charcoal (see above)

2 g agar

In a medium pot over medium heat, gently simmer the cream and vanilla bean charcoal for 10 minutes. Remove from the heat and, using an immersion blender, blend for approximately 15 seconds, until the vanilla beans are evenly distributed and incorporated into the liquid. The liquid will be gray rather than brown if the bean were charred correctly.

Using a chinois, fine-strain the vanilla bean cream into a measuring cup. Pour 1½ cups (375 ml) of the strained cream into the pot. Over medium heat, add the agar and bring the mixture to 200°F (93°C), then let simmer for just 5 seconds, to activate the agar. Pour into a container and let set on a flat surface at room temperature until firm to the touch, approximately 45 minutes.

Using an immersion blender, blend the mixture until smooth. Store in a squeeze bottle in the fridge for up to 5 days.

Vanilla Charcoal Ice Shards

Makes approximately 12

2 cups (500 ml) 10% cream

¾ oz (21 g) Vanilla Bean Charcoal (see left)

1 cup (185 g) dry ice pellets (see p. 6)

In a medium pot, gently simmer the cream and vanilla charcoal for 10 minutes. Remove from the heat. Using an immersion blender, blend for approximately 15 seconds, until the vanilla charcoal is fully incorporated into the cream.

Using a chinois, fine-strain into a half baking sheet and place on a flat surface in the freezer.

In a food processor, pulverize the dry ice pellets to a fine dust. Remove the sheet of frozen cream from the freezer and place on the countertop. Using a strainer, dust the vanilla charcoal cream with the dry ice dust to freeze.

Run a kitchen towel under warm water and spread out on the countertop. Place the baking sheet on top, to loosen the frozen cream from the sheet. Using an offset spatula, chip at the frozen cream to break off shards approximately 5 × 4 inches (13 × 10 cm) in size. Store in the freezer in an airtight container for up to 5 days.

White Chocolate and Pastis Bâtonnets

Makes approximately 12

- 5 oz (150 ml) 10% cream
- 5 oz (150 ml) water
- 2½ oz (75 ml) Pernod pastis
- 2¾ oz (75 g) Baker's white chocolate
- ¼ oz (6 g) agar
- 2 tsp (10 ml) Violet Fluid Gel (p. 63)

In a medium pot over low heat, heat the cream, water, pastis, chocolate, and agar, stirring constantly until the chocolate is melted. Bring the mixture to 200°F (93°C) and let simmer for 5 seconds. Strain into a 6 × 4-inch (15 × 10 cm) plastic container and let set on a flat surface at room temperature until firm to the touch, approximately 45 minutes. Square up the rounded corners of the hardened mixture, then cut into bâtonnets ¾ inch (2 cm) wide and 4 inches (10 cm) long. Store in a parchment paper–lined airtight container in the fridge for up to 3 days.

Balsam Fir Cream Gel

Makes approximately 1 cup (250 ml)

- 6¾ oz (200 ml) 10% cream
- 2 oz (60 ml) Balsam Fir Bitters (p. 16)
- 1 tbsp (12 g) white sugar
- 3 g agar

In a small pot over medium heat, bring the cream, bitters, sugar, and agar to 195°F (91°C) and let simmer for 3 seconds, to activate the agar. Remove from the heat and let set. Using an immersion blender, blend the mixture until smooth. Store in a squeeze bottle in the fridge for up to 3 days.

Violet Snow

Makes approximately 2 cups (500 ml)

- 6¾ oz (200 ml) water
- 6¾ oz (200 ml) violet liqueur
- 2 cups (370 g) dry ice pellets (see p. 6)

Pour the water and violet liqueur into a measuring container.

In a food processor, crush the dry ice pellets into a very fine dust, until the pieces are no larger than pea-sized, approximately 30 seconds. With the food processor on medium speed, slowly pour in the violet mixture. Turn off the food processor as soon as you have finished pouring. Store the snow in an airtight container in the freezer for up to 3 days.

Eucalyptus Shards

Makes approximately 12

- 2 cups (500 ml) water
- ¼ tsp (1 ml) organic food-grade eucalyptus essential oil

In a measuring container, stir the water and eucalyptus oil to mix. Pour into a half baking sheet and transfer to a flat surface in the freezer, freezing until 85% frozen. Hold the slab vertically over the sink to drain the water. Place on a flat surface and, using an offset spatula, chip at the slab to break off shards approximately 5 × 4 inches (13 × 10 cm) and in abstract shapes. Store in the freezer for up to 3 days.

Frozen White Chocolate and Balsam Fir Rosemary Sprig

Makes 1

Styrofoam container

1½ cups (375 ml) White Chocolate Water (p. 49)

2 oz (60 ml) Balsam Fir Bitters (p. 16)

One 6-inch (15 cm) rosemary sprig

8 cups (2 L) liquid nitrogen

In a measuring container, stir the white chocolate water and bitters to mix.

Prepare the rosemary sprig by ensuring the stem is as straight as possible and removing the leaves from the bottom 2 inches (5 cm), for easy handling.

Fill a Styrofoam container with the liquid nitrogen. Using tweezers, slowly submerge the rosemary sprig in the liquid nitrogen for 5 seconds. Remove and dip into the chocolate and bitters mixture. Dip into the liquid nitrogen again for 5 seconds. Repeat approximately 20 times, until ½ inch (1 cm) of ice forms on the rosemary. Store in an airtight container in the freezer for up to 3 days.

Eucalyptus Air

Makes approximately 8 cups (2 L)

8 cups (2 L) water

1 drop organic food-grade eucalyptus essential oil

1 g soy lecithin

1 egg white

In a deep bowl, use an immersion blender to blend the water, eucalyptus oil, soy lecithin, and egg white until the lecithin is dissolved and the egg white is thoroughly mixed in. Blend the surface of the mixture until it foams. Let set for 1 minute. Use immediately for serving and discard any leftovers.

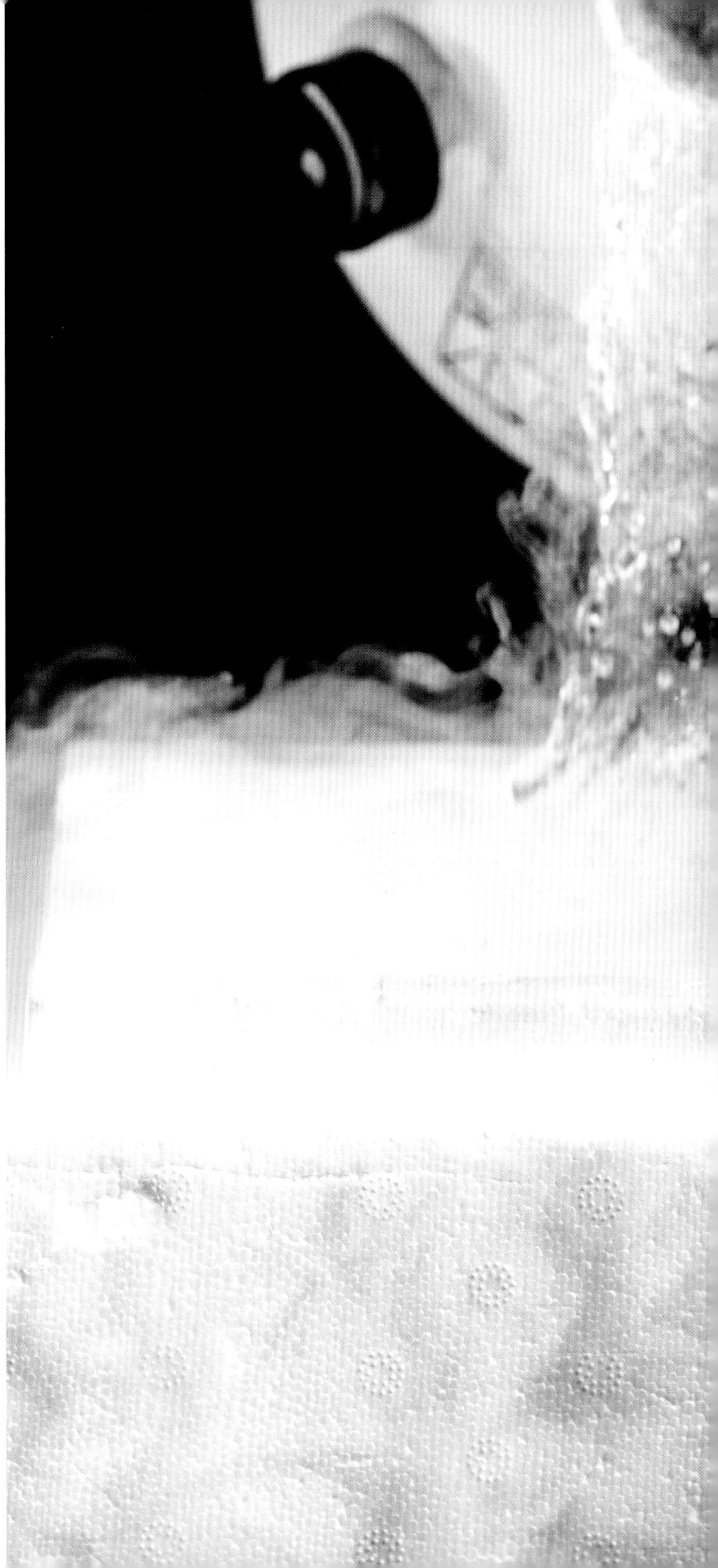

Inspired Sips

Like a winter walk in the forest, these cocktails echo the arboreal nature of Mezcal, White Chocolate, and Eucalyptus.

Winter Sour

Makes 1 • Glass: Coupe

2 oz (60 ml) pineapple juice
1 oz (30 ml) amaretto
1 oz (30 ml) Thyme Syrup (p. 21)
¾ oz (23 ml) fresh lemon juice
½ oz (15 ml) pastis
¼ oz (8 ml) Balsam Fir Bitters (p. 16)
1 egg white
Mint sprig, to garnish
Confectioners' sugar, for dusting

Put all the ingredients except the garnishes into a shaker, and dry shake to aerate the egg white. Fill the shaker with ice and shake for 2 seconds to chill. Using a fine cocktail strainer, strain into a coupe glass. Garnish with the mint sprig, then dust the mint with confectioners' sugar. Serve.

Spruce Gin and Pear

Makes 1 • Glass: Coupe

1¼ oz (38 ml) Spruce Tip Gin (p. 18)
½ oz (15 ml) pear liqueur
½ oz (15 ml) Thyme Syrup (p. 21)
¼ oz (8 ml) late harvest Vidal
2 oz (60 ml) elderflower soda
(I prefer Bottle Green)
Grapefruit peel, to garnish
Cedar sprig, to garnish
Confectioners' sugar, for dusting

Put the gin, pear liqueur, syrup, and Vidal into a mixing glass. Fill the mixing glass with ice and stir to chill, approximately three rotations. Using a cocktail strainer, fine-strain into a coupe glass. Pour in the elderflower soda. Gently squeeze the peel between your index finger and thumb to extract the oils into the cocktail. Discard the peel. Garnish with the cedar sprig, then dust with confectioners' sugar. Serve.

Muskoka

Makes 1 • Glass: Coupe

1¼ oz (38 ml) Canadian rye
¾ oz (23 ml) 10% cream
½ oz (15 ml) maple syrup
¼ oz (8 ml) amaretto
¼ oz (8 ml) Madeira
¼ oz (8 ml) Balsam Fir Bitters (p. 16)
Grated cinnamon, to garnish

Put all the ingredients except the cinnamon into a shaker. Fill the shaker with ice and shake for 2 seconds to chill. Using a fine cocktail strainer, strain into a coupe glass. Garnish with grated cinnamon.

Pictured opposite: Spruce Gin and Pear

Tsukiyama Garden

In Japanese, *tsukiyama* refers to a hill in a pond garden. I found the word to be a most fitting name for this cocktail that is inspired by the serenity of a Japanese pebble garden; the flow of a stream is replicated by the mist of the eucalyptus aromatics from the dry ice, cascading through the stones on the service piece, the leaves' fragrance evoking the outdoors. This cocktail reflects my multisensory approach to mixology; in it I've created visual texture and complexity with natural elements of eucalyptus, birch, and—to give a visual depth of field—river stones. There are also many progressive culinary techniques at play, including fat washing white chocolate water to produce the ice component, and the agar-based pearl technique that creates the delicious white chocolate and pastis ice drops. Nigori sake is also used for the ice cube component, as it tends to provide a softer, more floral flavor profile than other sake varietals; this lends beautiful levels of complexity to the transformative nature of this cocktail.

Makes 1
Glass: Stemless goblet

PLATING

- Approximately 25 medium river stones, thoroughly washed
- 1 hollowed birch or wooden service piece, approximately 14 inches (35 cm) in diameter
- Floral foam
- 1 battery-operated LED light
- Glass beads
- 8 various-length (3- to 6-inch/8 to 15 cm) pieces fresh baby blue eucalyptus

- 1 oz (30 ml) Absinthe Cream Fluid Gel (p. 176)
- 1 oz (30 ml) Black Licorice Fluid Gel (p. 176)
- 1 oz (30 ml) Green Cardamom Cream Fluid Gel (p. 177)
- 15 basil sprouts
- 1 Absinthe and Coconut Stone (p. 177)
- 3 tbsp (45 ml) Eucalyptus Crushed Ice (p. 177)
- 1 tbsp (15 ml) White Chocolate and Pastis Ice Drops (p. 177)
- 1 White Chocolate and Nigori Ice Cube (p. 176)
- 1 Balsam Fir Cream Encapsulation (p.178)
- 1-inch (2.5 cm) square edible silver leaf
- ¼ oz (8 ml) organic food-grade eucalyptus essential oil
- 2 dry ice pellets (see p. 6)
- 1 cup (250 ml) boiling water

COCKTAIL

Sake carafe (*tokkuri*)

- 1 oz (30 ml) coconut water
- ¾ oz (23 ml) white rum
- ½ oz (15 ml) coconut rum
- ¼ oz (8 ml) Thyme Syrup (p. 21)
- ¼ oz (8 ml) Green Cardamom Maraschino (p. 19)
- ¼ oz (8 ml) mezcal
- ⅛ oz (4 ml) pastis

To plate: Chill 5 river stones in the fridge.

Meanwhile, fill the birch service piece with the floral foam. Using a paring knife, cut out a 4-inch diameter circle in the floral foam for the LED light. Put in the LED light, along with the glass beads. Place the remaining 20 river stones and seven of the eucalyptus sprigs throughout the service piece to resemble a Japanese pebble garden.

Squeeze 4 dots of the absinthe cream gel, 6 dots of the black licorice gel, and 4 dots of the green cardamom gel on the river stones. Garnish 8 in total of the absinthe and the licorice gels with basil sprouts.

Place the absinthe and coconut stone at the 6 o'clock position on the birch service piece. Garnish with 1 basil sprout.

Place the eucalyptus crushed ice and the ice drops in a stemless goblet. Garnish the pearls with 2 dots of the licorice gel and 4 basil sprouts.

Place the nigori ice cube atop the crushed ice and pearls. Garnish with 2 dots of the absinthe gel, 2 dots of the licorice gel, and 2 basil spouts.

Arrange the chilled river stones throughout the front of the service piece. Place the balsam encapsulation on the chilled stones at 9 o'clock. Garnish with 1 dot of the licorice gel and the silver leaf.

Pour the eucalyptus oil into a small carafe and hide among the stones.

To compose the cocktail: Pour the cocktail ingredients into a mixing glass. Fill the mixing glass with ice and stir to chill, approximately three rotations. Using a cocktail strainer, fine-strain into the sake carafe.

continued

To serve: Add the dry ice and boiling water to the carafe holding the eucalyptus oil, causing vaporization and aromatics. Place the remaining eucalyptus sprig in the carafe. Pour the cocktail from the carafe into the goblet with the nigori sake and nigori ice cube.

White Chocolate and Nigori Ice Cube

Makes approximately 6 king cubes

King cube molds

4 cups (1 L) White Chocolate Water (p. 49)

2 cups (500 ml) nigori sake

In a measuring container, mix the white chocolate water with the nigori sake. Pour into king cube molds and freeze overnight. Store in a sealable container in the freezer for up to 5 days.

Absinthe Cream Fluid Gel

Makes approximately 1 cup (250 ml)

⅔ cup (150 ml) 10% cream

1¾ oz (50 ml) absinthe

1¾ oz (50 ml) Thyme Syrup (p. 21)

5 g agar

In a medium pot over medium heat, bring all the ingredients to 195°F (91°C) and let simmer for 3 seconds, to activate the agar. Pour into a glass bowl and let set on a flat surface at room temperature until firm to the touch, approximately 30 minutes. Using an immersion blender, blend the mixture until smooth. Store in a squeeze bottle in the fridge for up to 3 days.

Black Licorice Fluid Gel

Makes approximately 1 cup (250 ml)

6¾ oz (200 ml) water

6¾ oz (200 ml) black sambuca

4.5 g agar

In a small pot, bring all the ingredients to 195°F (91°C) and let simmer for 3 seconds, to activate the agar. Pour into a glass bowl and let set on a flat surface at room temperature until firm to the touch, approximately 30 minutes. Using an immersion blender, blitz until smooth. Store in a squeeze bottle in the fridge for up to 3 days.

Green Cardamom Cream Fluid Gel

Makes approximately 1½ cups (375 ml)

- 5 oz (150 ml) Green Cardamom Maraschino (p. 19)
- 7 tbsp (105 ml) 10% cream
- ¼ cup (60 ml) water
- 3 g agar

In a medium pot over medium heat, bring all the ingredients to 195°F (91°C) and let simmer for 3 seconds, to activate the agar. Transfer to a glass bowl and let set on a flat surface at room temperature until firm to the touch, 30 minutes. Using an immersion blender, blend the mixture until smooth. Store in a squeeze bottle in the fridge for up to 3 days.

Absinthe and Coconut Stones

Makes approximately 12

Twelve 1-inch (2.5 cm) demisphere molds

- 1 cup (250 ml) coconut water
- 1¾ oz (50 ml) absinthe
- 1¾ oz (50 ml) coconut rum
- 1¾ oz (50 ml) Thyme Syrup (p. 21)
- 3 g agar

In a small pot over medium heat, stir all the ingredients together until the agar is dissolved. Bring to 200°F (93°C) and let simmer for 3 seconds, to activate the agar. Carefully pour into the demisphere molds and let set on a flat surface at room temperature, approximately 30 minutes. Remove the demispheres from the molds. Store in a parchment paper–lined airtight container in the fridge for up to 3 days.

Eucalyptus Crushed Ice

Makes approximately 4 cups (1 L)

- 4 cups (1 L) ice cubes
- 2 drops organic food-grade eucalyptus essential oil

In a food processor, pulverize the ice and oil until combined and crushed. Store in an airtight container in the freezer for up to 3 days.

White Chocolate and Pastis Ice Drops

Makes approximately 1½ cups (375 ml)

Styrofoam container

- 5 oz (150 ml) 10% cream
- 5 oz (150 ml) water
- 2½ oz (75 g) Baker's white chocolate
- 2½ oz (75 ml) Pernod pastis
- ¼ oz (6 g) agar
- 8 cups (2 L) liquid nitrogen

In a small pot over medium heat, stir together the cream, water, white chocolate, pastis, and agar. Bring to 200°F (93°C) and let simmer for 3 seconds, to activate the agar. Pour into a squeeze bottle.

Fill a Styrofoam container with the liquid nitrogen. From 1 foot (30 cm) above the container, carefully squeeze drops of the mixture into the liquid nitrogen. Carefully drain the nitrogen. Separate the pearls and store in an airtight container in the freezer for up to 3 days.

Balsam Fir Cream Encapsulations

Makes approximately 12

Twenty-four 1-inch (2.5 cm) demisphere molds

⅔ cup (150 ml) 10% cream

1¼ oz (38 ml) Balsam Fir Bitters (p. 16)

2 tbsp (30 ml) water

2 tbsp (30 ml) Pernod pastis

1 g xanthan gum

7 oz (200 g) cacao butter

6 oz (170 g) white chocolate

To make the filling, using an immersion blender, blend the cream, bitters, water, pastis, and xanthan gum in a measuring container until evenly distributed and smooth. Pour into a third pan and let sit to remove the air bubbles, approximately 30 minutes.

Fill the demisphere molds with the filling. Place on a flat surface in the freezer and freeze for 2 hours, or until frozen solid.

Remove the frozen fillings from their molds. Hold one piece in each hand and, using a ceramic plate, rub the flat side of the demisphere on it to smooth into a flat, even edge. Hold the flat sides of the two demispheres together and run your fingertip along the seam to seal them and smooth out any imperfections. Store in an airtight container in the freezer to maintain their shape.

To make the encapsulation casings, prepare a double boiler: place a stainless-steel bowl atop a small pot filled with water over medium heat (the bowl should be the same circumference as the pan). Melt the cacao butter and white chocolate in the bowl, stirring frequently to evenly incorporate the ingredients. Keep warm.

Poke a pin into a frozen sphere and submerge twice in the melted cacao butter to thoroughly coat. Remove the pin and place the sphere in a demisphere mold to maintain its shape. Repeat with the remaining spheres. Gently scrape a paring knife along where the pin was to remove excess chocolate. Using a pin, dip the tip into the melted cocoa butter mixture and fill the hole. Store in an airtight container in the fridge for up to 3 days. Let sit at room temperature for 30 minutes before serving.

Inspired Sips

These crisp sips are inspired by the nature-set Tsukiyama Garden.

Grapefruit and Eucalyptus Paloma

Makes 1 • Glass: Collins

1 cup (250 ml) Eucalyptus Crushed Ice (p. 177)
1½ oz (45 ml) reposado tequila
½ oz (15 ml) St-Germain
½ oz (15 ml) Madeira
¼ oz (8 ml) Thyme Syrup (p. 21)
2 oz (60 ml) sparkling grapefruit soda
Grapefruit peel, to garnish
Eucalyptus stem, to garnish

Fill a collins glass with the eucalyptus crushed ice.

Pour the tequila, St-Germain, Madeira, and syrup into a mixing glass. Fill the mixing glass with ice and stir to chill, approximately three rotations. Using a fine cocktail strainer, strain over the eucalyptus ice in the collins glass. Top with the sparkling grapefruit soda. Gently squeeze the peel between your index finger and thumb to extract the oils into the cocktail. Discard the peel. Garnish with the eucalyptus stem. Serve.

Evergreen Silk and Satin

Makes 1 • Glass: Double old-fashioned

1 White Chocolate and Nigori Ice Cube (p. 176)
2 oz (60 ml) coconut rum
¼ oz (8 ml) Green Cardamom Maraschino (p. 19)
¼ oz (8 ml) Madeira
¼ oz (8 ml) Balsam Fir Bitters (p. 16)
2 grapefruit peels, to garnish

Put the white chocolate and nigori ice cube into a double old-fashioned glass.

Pour the coconut rum, maraschino, Madeira, and bitters into a mixing glass. Fill the mixing glass with ice and stir to chill. Using a cocktail strainer, fine-strain over the nigori ice cube in the double old-fashioned glass. Gently squeeze 1 peel between your index finger and thumb to extract the oils into the cocktail. Garnish the ice with the remaining grapefruit peel. Serve.

Winter Mezcal

Makes 1 • Glass: Double old-fashioned

1½ oz (45 ml) mezcal
¼ oz (8 ml) Thyme Syrup (p. 21)
¼ oz (8 ml) Balsam Fir Bitters (p. 16)
¼ oz (8 ml) late harvest Vidal
⅛ oz (4 ml) absinthe
King ice cube
Grapefruit peel, to garnish

Put the mezcal, syrup, bitters, Vidal, and absinthe into a shaker. Fill the shaker with ice and stir to chill, approximately three rotations. Using a cocktail strainer, fine-strain into a double old-fashioned glass over a king ice cube. Gently squeeze the peel between your index finger and thumb to extract the oils into the cocktail. Discard the peel. Serve.

Pictured opposite: Winter Mezcal

Winter Cider

An elevated take on the iconic seasonal hot apple cider, this cocktail is another favorite of mine and the epitome of winter. The caramel ice vessel provides a rich texture and structure at the beginning of your experience, gradually balancing the "heat" of the alcohol and ginger as it melts into the final flavor composition. Once the caramel ice bowl is fully melted, the result is both rich and complex, with beautiful structure and balance. The caraway salt gives additional levels of complexity with its smoky and savory quality. The brunoise-cut apples bring a natural pop of texture and taste, pairing nicely with the fabricated cinnamon brunoise and the fluid gels, which release their flavors in exciting bursts. As the ice melts, the transformative flavor profile creates a cocktail that evolves over time.

Makes 1
Glass: Tall glass bowl

COCKTAIL

- 4 oz (120 ml) unfiltered apple cider
- 2 oz (60 ml) rye
- ½ oz (15 ml) Amaro Lucano

PLATING

- 1 tall glass bowl

- 2 tbsp (30 ml) Bitter Almond Snow (p. 184)
- 2 tbsp (30 ml) Ginger and Vanilla Snow (p. 184)
- 1 tsp (5 ml) Cinnamon Brunoise (p. 184)
- 1 tbsp (15 ml) Fernet and Vanilla Fluid Gel (p. 184)
- 3 mint sprigs (1 medium and 2 small), to garnish
- One 1 × 2-inch (2.5 × 5 cm) cinnamon stick
- 1 Caramel Ice Bowl (p. 185)
- 1 Granny Smith apple, cut into ¼-inch (6 mm) cubes
- 1 pinch Caraway Salt (p. 184)
- ½ oz (15 ml) Maple and Madeira Fluid Gel (p. 126)
- Star anise pod, to garnish

To compose the cocktail: In a small pot over low heat, stir together all the cocktail ingredients, bring to a gentle simmer, and then set aside.

To plate: Meanwhile, in a glass bowl, place 2 tbsp (30 ml) each of the almond snow and the ginger and vanilla snow. Add the brunoise and 4 dots of the fernet and vanilla gel. Garnish with the medium mint sprig and the cinnamon stick.

Place the caramel ice bowl atop the mouth of a tall glass bowl.

Put 1 tbsp of the cubed apples in the caramel ice bowl. Sprinkle with the caraway salt. Squeeze approximately 15 dots of the maple and Madeira gel overtop, and garnish with the small mint sprigs and star anise.

To serve: Pour the still-warm cocktail into the caramel ice bowl. The ice bowl will melt slowly, allowing all the components to mix, to create the finished flavor profile of the cocktail.

Caraway Salt

Makes approximately 3 tbsp (45 ml)

- 2 tbsp (30 ml) smoked Maldon salt
- 1 tbsp (15 ml) caraway seeds

Using a mortar and pestle, grind the Maldon salt and caraway seeds into a fine dust. Store in an airtight container at room temperature. The salt will last and maintain its flavor profile indefinitely.

Cinnamon Brunoise

Makes approximately 1½ cups (375 ml)

- 10 oz (300 ml) Cinnamon Syrup (p. 20)
- 3½ oz (105 ml) water
- 4 g agar

In a small pot over medium heat, bring the syrup, water, and agar to 203°F (95°C) and let simmer for 5 seconds, to activate the agar. Pour into a half pan and let set on a flat surface at room temperature for 60 minutes, or until firm to the touch. Remove from the pan and cut into ¼-inch (6 mm) cubes. Store in an airtight container in the fridge for up to 5 days.

Bitter Almond Snow

Makes approximately 2 cups (500 ml)

- 1½ cups (375 ml) water
- 7 tbsp (105 ml) amaretto
- 2 cups (370 g) dry ice pellets (see p. 6)

Pour the water and amaretto into a measuring container.

In a food processor, crush the dry ice pellets into a very fine dust, until the pieces are no larger than pea-sized, approximately 30 seconds. With the food processor on medium speed, slowly pour in the amaretto mixture. Turn off the food processor as soon as you have finished pouring. Store the snow in an airtight container in the freezer for up to 3 days.

Ginger and Vanilla Snow

Makes approximately 2 cups (500 ml)

- 1½ cups (375 ml) water
- 7 tbsp (105 ml) Vanilla Syrup (p. 21)
- ¼ cup (60 ml) fresh ginger juice
- 2 cups (370 g) dry ice pellets (see p. 6)

Pour the water, syrup, and ginger juice into a measuring container.

In a food processor, crush the dry ice pellets into a very fine dust, until the pieces are no larger than pea-sized, approximately 30 seconds. With the food processor on medium speed, slowly pour in the ginger mixture. Turn off the food processor as soon as you have finished pouring. Store the snow in an airtight container in the freezer for up to 3 days.

Fernet and Vanilla Fluid Gel

Makes approximately 1 cup (250 ml)

- ¾ cup (175 ml) water
- 2½ oz (75 ml) Vanilla Syrup (p. 21)
- 1¾ oz (50 ml) Fernet-Branca
- 3.5 g agar

In a medium pot over medium heat, bring all the ingredients to 201°F (94°C). Pour into a steel container and let set on a flat surface at room temperature until firm to the touch, approximately 1 hour. Using an immersion blender, blend the mixture until smooth. Store in a squeeze bottle in the fridge for up to 3 days.

Caramel Ice Bowls

Makes 2

1 oz (30 ml) steel ladle

2½ cups (625 ml) water

1½ cups (102 g) white sugar

¼ cup (60 ml) 10% cream

2 cups (370 g) dry ice pellets (see p. 6)

Pour the water into an airtight container. Leave unsealed and set aside.

In a medium pot over low heat, heat the sugar to caramelize it; avoid stirring so as to reduce crystallization, but make sure it doesn't burn.

In a small pot over low heat, bring the cream to a gentle simmer. Slowly add the cream to the caramelized sugar, stirring constantly—be careful, as there will be a boiling reaction due to the contrast of the ingredients' temperatures.

Pour the caramel into the prepared water container and stir to fully incorporate. Let cool, then store sealed in the fridge for up to 3 days. (Feel free to freeze any remaining caramel water in ice molds; caramel ice cubes work beautifully in your favorite Old-Fashioned or Manhattan recipe.)

In a food processor, crush the dry ice pellets into a very fine dust, until the pieces are no larger than pea-sized, approximately 30 seconds. Fill the ladle with the pulverized dry ice to freeze the ladle. Slowly dip the ladle into the caramel water for 1 second to coat the outside of the ladle up to ¾ inch (2 cm) from the lip, then remove the ladle and hold in the air to allow the caramel water to freeze on it. Once frozen, resubmerge the ladle to create another layer of ice level with the first layer. Repeat the process until the ice bowl is approximately ¼ inch (6 mm) thick.

Pour out the dry ice from the ladle and fill the ladle with tepid water, so that it is warm enough to use your fingers to slowly remove the ice bowl. Repeat this entire process with the remaining caramel water; you should have enough to make two bowls. Store in the freezer for up to 3 days.

Inspired Sips

The Winter Cider spreads its warmth in these cocktails with notes of ginger, apple cider, and cinnamon.

Spiced Cider Spritz

Makes 1 • Glass: Large highball

- 3 oz (90 ml) apple cider
- 1¾ oz (50 ml) Canadian rye
- ¾ oz (23 ml) Cinnamon Syrup (p. 20)
- ¼ oz (8 ml) Fernet-Branca
- 2 mint sprigs
- 2 oz (60 ml) soda water
- Confectioners' sugar, for dusting

Put the apple cider, rye, syrup, Fernet-Branca, and leaves from 1 mint sprig in a large highball glass. Muddle. Fill the glass with ice and stir to chill, approximately three rotations. Add the soda water. Garnish with the remaining mint sprig, then dust the mint with confectioners' sugar. Serve.

Oud

Makes 1 • Glass: Collins

- 1¾ oz (50 ml) Cedar Rye (p. 19)
- 1¼ oz (38 ml) Star Anise Syrup (p. 21)
- ½ oz (15 ml) Balsam Fir Bitters (p. 16)
- ½ oz (15 ml) Caraway Maraschino (p. 19)
- ¼ oz (8 ml) Saffron Brandy (p. 18)
- 2 oz (60 ml) ginger beer
- Tied wheat and cedar, to garnish
- Orange peel, to garnish

Pour the rye, syrup, bitters, maraschino, and brandy over ice in a collins glass. Pour the ginger beer overtop. Stir to incorporate. Garnish with the tied wheat and cedar. Gently squeeze the peel between your index finger and thumb to extract the oils into the cocktail. Discard the peel. Serve.

Winter Harvest

Makes 1 • Glass: Coupe

- 1 oz (30 ml) bourbon
- ½ oz (15 ml) Islay Scotch
- ¼ oz (8 ml) amaretto
- ¼ oz (8 ml) Cinnamon Syrup (p. 20)
- ¼ oz (8 ml) Balsam Fir Bitters (p. 16)
- ¼ oz (8 ml) sweet vermouth
- Orange peel, to garnish

Put all the ingredients except the orange peel into a mixing glass. Fill the mixing glass with ice and stir to chill, approximately three rotations. Using a fine cocktail strainer, strain into a coupe glass. Gently squeeze the peel between your index finger and thumb to extract the oils into the cocktail. Discard the peel. Serve.

Pictured opposite: Oud

Winter Storm

This cocktail was born when a popular whisky brand commissioned me to create a menu for its cross-Canada tour of exclusive tasting events. We brought BarChef's modernist mixology experience across the country, creating the immersive kinds of experiences we pride ourselves on. This Winter Storm cocktail ended up being so highly lauded that we carved out a place for it on BarChef's winter menu. When placed in front of the guest, it has the element of temperature by way of a cold breeze from the juniper branch submerged in liquid nitrogen. This sensation is further enhanced with the cryo-poached meringue lending a "winter's breath" effect with tones of absinthe and balsam fir.

Makes 1
Glass: Crystal cognac

COCKTAIL

Serving carafe

- 1¾ oz (50 ml) Highland Scotch
- ¼ oz (8 ml) Thyme Syrup (p. 21)
- ¼ oz (8 ml) Balsam Fir Bitters (p. 16)
- ⅛ oz (4 ml) absinthe

PLATING

Styrofoam container

- 3 tbsp (45 ml) Maple and Madeira Snow (p. 190)
- 1 piece Vidal Rosemary Ice Shard (p. 191)
- 3 Meringue Shards (p. 191)
- 1 Absinthe and Balsam Fir Essence (p. 190)
- 8 cups (2 L) liquid nitrogen
- 2 pinches Candy Floss (p. 191)
- 1 juniper branch, approximately 16 inches (40 cm) long

To compose the cocktail: Pour all the cocktail ingredients into a mixing glass. Fill the mixing glass with ice and stir to chill, approximately three rotations. Using a fine cocktail strainer, strain into a carafe and set aside.

To plate: Place the snow in a cognac glass, then place the rosemary ice shard on top.

Spray the meringue shards with two spritzes of the absinthe and balsam fir essence. Fill a Styrofoam container with the liquid nitrogen. Using tongs, carefully submerge the meringue shards in the liquid nitrogen and leave submerged for 20 seconds.

To serve: Pour the cocktail into the cognac glass, over the snow and frozen rosemary.

Place the candy floss on the rosemary and spray with two spritzes of the absinthe and balsam fir essence from approximately 1 foot (30 cm) above the service piece.

Using tongs, fully submerge the juniper branch in the liquid nitrogen for 20 seconds. Remove and place aside. Place the ice shards upright in the center of the frozen juniper branch. Present the branch to your guest, alongside the cocktail.

Absinthe and Balsam Fir Essence

Makes approximately 1 cup (250 ml)

Atomizer

3½ oz (105 ml) French absinthe

6¾ oz (200 ml) Balsam Fir Bitters (p. 16)

Pour the absinthe and bitters into an atomizer. Shake to incorporate. Store at room temperature. The essence will last indefinitely.

Maple and Madeira Snow

Makes approximately 1½ cups (375 ml)

6¾ oz (200 ml) Madeira

6¾ oz (200 ml) water

3½ oz (105 ml) maple syrup

2 cups (370 g) dry ice pellets (see p. 6)

Pour the Madeira, water, and maple syrup into a measuring container.

In a food processor, crush the dry ice pellets into a very fine dust, until the pieces are no larger than pea-sized, approximately 30 seconds. With the food processor on medium speed, slowly pour in the Madeira mixture. Turn off the food processor as soon as you have finished pouring. Store the snow in an airtight container in the freezer for up to 3 days.

Vidal Rosemary Ice Shard

Makes approximately 10 pieces

Styrofoam container

6¾ oz (200 ml) water

5 oz (150 ml) late harvest Vidal

Ten 4-inch (10 cm) rosemary sprigs

8 cups (2 L) liquid nitrogen

Pour the water and Vidal into a cylindrical vessel deep enough to submerge the rosemary sprig. Set this bath aside.

Fill a Styrofoam container with the liquid nitrogen. Using tongs, submerge the rosemary upside down in the liquid nitrogen, to fan out the leaves. Remove once the bubbling subsides, after approximately 5 seconds. Submerge the frozen rosemary in the Vidal bath for 1 second, then again submerge the rosemary in the liquid nitrogen for 3 seconds, and again in the Vidal bath for 3 seconds. Repeat this process 12 times to create a thick layer of ice over the rosemary sprig, so that it resembles a snow-covered fir tree. Repeat with the remaining 9 rosemary sprigs.

Store in an airtight container in the freezer for up to 3 days.

Meringue Shards

Makes approximately 20

6 egg whites

1½ cups (102 g) white sugar

Preheat the oven to 150°F (65°C). Line a baking sheet with a Silpat.

In a large mixing bowl, using a hand blender on low speed, whisk the egg whites while slowly adding the sugar, until light and frothy. Spoon the meringue onto the prepared baking sheet.

Using a large offset spatula, flatten the mixture to approximately ½ inch (1 cm) depth. Bake for 40 minutes, then rotate the pan and bake for another 40 minutes. Remove and let cool to room temperature.

Use your hands to carefully remove the meringue pieces from the pan, creating golf ball-sized shards. Store in an airtight container at room temperature for up to 3 days.

Candy Floss

Makes 4 cups (1 L)

Candy floss machine

Plastic cones

2 tbsp (24 g) white sugar

Turn on the candy floss machine and let it reach temperature. Turn off the machine. Using a spoon, put the sugar into the center steel ring. Turn the machine on. Holding a plastic cone or wooden spoon, circle the circumference of the machine's steel ring while rotating, to gather a softball-sized amount of candy floss. Transfer to a dry stainless-steel bowl (it's very important that the bowl is dry so that the candy floss doesn't absorb moisture) and cover with plastic wrap. Store at room temperature for up to 3 days.

Inspired Sips

Get a taste of the Winter Storm's iconic absinthe and balsam fir dragon's breath with each sip of these drinks.

Winter Scotch Flip

Makes 1 • Glass: Coupe

1½ oz (45 ml) Highland Scotch
1 oz (30 ml) maple syrup
½ oz (15 ml) pastis
¼ oz (8 ml) amaretto
¼ oz (8 ml) Balsam Fir Bitters (p. 16)
1 egg
1 piece cedar

Put all the ingredients except the cedar in a shaker. Fill the shaker with ice and shake for 5 seconds to chill the mixture. Using a fine cocktail strainer, strain into a coupe glass. Garnish with the cedar. Serve.

Winter Solstice

Makes 1 • Glass: Double old-fashioned

1¼ oz (38 ml) Spruce Tip Gin (p. 18)
½ oz (15 ml) Madeira
½ oz (15 ml) Thyme Syrup (p. 21)
¼ oz (8 ml) Balsam Fir Bitters (p. 16)
King ice cube
Grapefruit peel, to garnish
Eucalyptus leaf, to garnish

Pour the gin, Madeira, syrup, and bitters into a mixing glass. Fill the mixing glass with ice and stir to chill. Using a Hawthorne strainer, fine-strain into a double old-fashioned glass over a king cube. Gently squeeze the peel between your index finger and thumb to extract the oils into the cocktail. Discard the peel. Garnish the ice with the eucalyptus leaf. Serve.

Niagara Spritz

Makes 1 • Glass: White wine

2 oz (60 ml) Late Harvest Vidal
2 oz (60 ml) apple cider
¼ oz (8 ml) amaretto
¼ oz (8 ml) St-Germain
⅛ oz (4 ml) absinthe
3 oz (90 ml) sparkling wine
Cinnamon stick, to garnish
Mint crown, to garnish

Pour the Vidal, apple cider, amaretto, elderflower liqueur, and absinthe into a white wine glass. Fill the glass with ice and stir to chill for 3 seconds. Top with the sparkling wine. Garnish with the cinnamon and mint. Serve.

Pictured opposite: Winter Solstice

ACKNOWLEDGMENTS

Thank you to the entire team at Frankie Solarik Holdings: your hard work and dedication is humbling and truly appreciated. Directors Kurt Tissera, Lionel Duke, and Gianluca Passuello, your passion and loyalty is a driving factor of all our concepts' success, and I am truly grateful and humbled to work alongside you as we strive to achieve our company objectives and goals! Also a huge thank-you to all the fantastic guests who have joined us at BarChef over the years—the whole reason I do what I do. I want to create an entirely new perspective to the possibilities of the cocktail experience, and I truly hope your experiences at our venues have elevated your expectations with this amazing medium. Thank you!

Jan. 26.18
Lavender

INDEX

Note: Cocktails and sub-recipes are listed under both ingredients and flavor profiles.

C

D

E

F

G

H

I

J

K

L

R

S

T

V

W

X